NEFARIOUS

NEFARIOUS
A LIFE IN CRIME

RONNIE FIELD
& MARTIN KNIGHT

HARPER
element

HarperElement
An imprint of HarperCollins*Publishers*
1 London Bridge Street
London SE1 9GF

www.harpercollins.co.uk

HarperCollins*Publishers*
Macken House, 39/40 Mayor Street Upper
Dublin 1, D01 C9W8, Ireland

First published by HarperElement 2024

1 3 5 7 9 10 8 6 4 2

© Ronnie Field and Martin Knight 2024

Ronnie Field and Martin Knight assert the moral right
to be identified as the authors of this work

Plate-section images courtesy of the Field family collection,
Kate Kray (images on plate 3) and Charles Bronson
(illustration at the top of plate 6)

A catalogue record of this book is
available from the British Library

ISBN 978-0-00-865903-5

Printed and bound in the UK using 100%
renewable electricity at CPI Group (UK) Ltd

'The money was good, the hours were short, but the holidays were very long.'

'I'd like to thank National Westminster Bank,
Midland Bank, Barclays Bank and Lloyds Bank,
without whom none of this would have
been possible ...'

Ronnie Field opens his father-of-the-bride speech
at his daughter's wedding

Ronnie Field would like to dedicate this book to
his mother, Vera Elizabeth Smith (1909–1968).

Martin Knight would like to dedicate this book
to his uncle, Terry Bradshaw (1924–2017).
A Battersea boy.

CONTENTS

FOREWORD

Twenty-something years ago I was invited by some friends one hot summer's evening to meet them for a drink in Tone's Bar in Cheam. Although the place was local to me, I wasn't a regular. When I got there, one of my pals directed me to a stool in the corner of the bar and invited me to take a seat. I hopped on and tucked into my first early-evening Guinness. Soon a man entered, and the throng around the bar area parted as he headed my way. He was a handsome, striking man who looked to be in his late fifties to early sixties, had silver swept-back hair, a flowery summer shirt, sun-browned leathery skin, with a chunky identity bracelet on his wrist and a medallion around his neck. To me he resembled an American Italian Mafia figure straight from a De Niro movie. I wasn't far wrong. This was Joey Pyle, but I didn't know it yet. Following in his wake was a black guy who it would require a step ladder for the average man to achieve eye-level communication with.

Joe stopped in front of me. The bar and my friends fell worryingly silent. They had that look that said, 'You've done it now.'

'You're in my chair,' Joe said calmly, his hands on his hips, looking at me.

I practically jumped off and quickly apologised, brushing the seat down after me. Joe broke into a big grin, extended his hand and everyone had a good laugh at my expense. It was a set-up.

I met Joe several times after. He had a book out and wondered if I'd like to do another with him. He wasn't happy with the first, he said. I explained it would be unusual and difficult to publish two autobiographies in as many years. He spoke mostly about boxing and especially American heavyweight champions, some of whom he knew. I found him warm, funny and interesting. Never in front of me did he discuss any gangsterism.

One day he called me and asked me to meet him in the Beverley Brook, a pub closer to where he lived. He said he had something to show me. I was curious and a little trepidatious at the same time. When I got there he was alone, which was unusual. He called over a member of the pub staff. Joe didn't go to the bar; the bar went to him. When I settled down next to him the thought went through my mind, what if one of his mortal enemies – all crime bosses have mortal enemies, don't they? – came to assassinate him? Would they shoot me as well?

Joe proceeded to show me some poems he had written. He wanted to know what I thought of them.

'Give me your honest opinion. If they're shit, I want you to tell me.'

I sat there and read them in front of him.

'Well?'

'They're good, Joe. Really good. But … I don't know much about poetry.'

'That's good enough for me.'

Through Joe I met a close pal of his called Del, who was an admirer of my book *Battersea Girl*, having been brought up in the area. Del wanted to introduce me to a man called Ronnie Field. 'He's got a great life story and I think you could do a pukka book together,' assured Del. I knew Ronnie's name; he was one of those almost mythical people talked about in pubs who you never actually saw. At least I didn't. I vaguely knew he was close to Joey Pyle and had a big reputation.

Del took me to meet Ronnie in a social club hidden behind some residential houses over St Helier way. He was a solid chap in his mid-fifties with a firm handshake who laughed and joked a lot. I found him very funny. However, he hadn't long been released from prison and I sensed he was focused on living his life, not writing about it. Besides which, I'd just finished writing George Best's book and had launched straight into Dave Mackay's. It wasn't the time.

Twenty years later it was. I joined my pals Jimmy and Wally Stockins and Gypsy Joe Smith on a trip over to Raynes Park to have a drink with Del and Ronnie. Ronnie was older, quieter and more reflective than at our previous meeting, which, of course, he didn't remember. Ronnie and I chatted on the edge of the group, which got louder and louder as the John Smith's flowed. Some of the memories he shared that evening fascinated me. Joe Smith, who doesn't miss a trick, shouted over.

'Why don't you do Ronnie's book, Martin?'

'If he wants to,' I replied. What else could I say?

We shook hands there and then.

I've always wanted to write a true-crime book, and this was my opportunity. I co-wrote a book called *Grass* with Martin King and Phil Sparrowhawk – telling of the exploits of Phil and Howard Marks, his partner in drug smuggling – which I loved doing, but it was that 1960s and 1970s London underworld I'd always wanted to delve into since I started writing, as my childhood had coincided with the Great Train Robbery, Harry Roberts, and the trials of the Richardsons and the Krays.

At my comprehensive school in the 1970s, reading books for most schoolboys was only undertaken under duress, as part of the educational curriculum. There were far more exciting things to do as a teenager. Two books did get widely read, however: *Skinhead* by Richard Allen and *The Profession of Violence* by John Pearson. One was the fictional adventures of a violent skinhead thug called Joe Hawkins, the other the story of the Kray twins, real-life gangsters from London's East End. Both books, crumpled and dog-eared, were passed from boy to boy and read surreptitiously in lessons, the risk of confiscation and a smack around the head always present. When the skinhead phenomenon passed, the Allen book slid into obscurity, but Pearson's study elevated the Kray twins into mainstream folklore and propelled a previously marginal literary genre into the big time. Half a century later Ronnie and Reggie are still a British obsession, and new books about them appear every year.

This isn't one of them. This is the story of Ronnie Field, a south London armed robber. His criminal trajectory did overlap with the twins, and they became good friends, and the denouement of Ronnie's criminal career was being Charlie Kray's co-defendant following an undercover police operation. So, Kray brothers do figure in Ronnie's story, Charlie especially. But I believe *Nefarious* provides an insight into the criminal world in a less obvious part of the capital, where south London meets the suburbs. Ronnie Field reveals how an innocent little boy in Cheam in leafy Surrey ended up robbing banks, being affiliated with Joey Pyle and spending too many of his first fifty-plus years on the planet in prison. Ronnie doesn't attempt to justify or glorify anything. It's what happened to him, and he hopes that his life may be of interest to others, be they true-crime enthusiasts or those who simply enjoy working-class social history. Ronnie's one of the last men standing who lived in that now fast-disappearing criminal world. Armed robbers of banks, post offices and industrial premises seem almost as dated as highwaymen. The world has changed and so has crime. As to whether the change has been for the better – the jury's out.

Martin Knight
August 2023

1

WE ARE FAMILY

My childhood was shit. I was one of the last workhouse babies, for starters. At least, I hope I was. The workhouse was the ever-present looming threat hovering above the working classes that dominated their fears and stalked their sleep. For many it was considered a result to live a life that didn't involve entering the workhouse at one time or another. It was the last resort for food and shelter for the poverty-stricken, the destitute and the fragile. They called people like us paupers. Not very nice.

Inmates of the workhouse were expected to carry out menial labour in exchange for their basic shelter and grub. Hence the name – work and house. It was gruelling, humiliating and soul-destroying. The shame of turning to the workhouse in times of trouble passed down the generations like a guilty secret. Thankfully, it's no longer a grim feature of our social landscape. Although mainly associated in the public mind with the Victorian era, workhouses nevertheless endured well into the twentieth century and only finally completely disappeared from our lives with the coming of the National Health Service in the late 1940s. Good job I don't remember it.

My mother Vera gave birth to me in the workhouse in Epsom in Surrey. Workhouses co-existing with the large, plush houses of the stockbroker belt is a strange fact. I was her final child of seven, not including others that sadly died in pregnancy and childbirth. In order of arrival, Pat came first in 1933, then Billy, Ted, Cissy, Dalla and Peter, and finally me on 9 August 1946. Jimmy, our cousin, also lived with us. I was never sure why. He was my father's sister's boy and a smashing kid. When he grew up, he joined the navy and served on the *Ark Royal*. Dalla was adopted out early on. She was brought back to see us occasionally by her new parents but didn't live at home. This sounds like quite a harsh arrangement, but it may be that Dalla was the lucky one.

On my birth certificate under 'When and where born' it states 49 Dorking Road, Epsom, which was the address of the Epsom Union Workhouse. By this time, the authorities had decided to disguise reality by no longer stating 'workhouse' on birth, marriage and death certificates in a rare empathetic effort not to stigmatise people for life. I understand that I was only in there for my birth and my mum's immediate recovery, but she was a regular visitor and my eldest sibling, my dear Pat, who was thirteen years older than me, can remember being in there for longer periods with her and other brothers and sisters at various times. Today the bustling Epsom General Hospital, which the old workhouse morphed into, sprawls across the site and very few people remain that are witness to its miserable and sad past.

When I was born in 1946, large-scale social events were being resumed for the first time since the Second World War. A horse called Airborne won the Derby on the other side of Banstead from us up on Epsom Downs, and in football Derby County beat Charlton in the first FA Cup final for six years. To really underline the fact that the war was over, the Nuremberg Trials had kicked off. Nazi war criminals were being judged and hanged or, in the case of Himmler and Goering, biting into a cyanide capsule in a final and dramatic act of defiance. Those that could afford to go to the Century cinema, just up from our house in Cheam village, or the bigger Granada in North Cheam, would be getting steamed up watching Hollywood's *The Postman Always Ring Twice*, starring the sultry and voluptuous Lana Turner, or our home-grown *George in Civvy Street*, featuring gormless George Formby. Tommy Handley put smiles on war-weary faces over the airwaves with his hugely popular radio show *ITMA* (*It's That Man Again*). Jack Straw, Bill Clinton and Keith Moon were all born within a few days of me. I guess Straw, a future Home Secretary, was the only one who influenced my life in any way.

Researching my family tree for this book has thrown up some interesting facts. I knew that one of my grandfathers was an agricultural labourer on the farmland that would become the site of the St Helier hospital and estate. I didn't know, though, that a great-grandfather on my paternal side,

Elijah Chatt, was probably an English Romany gypsy. The census reveals that as a boy he had an address as Ash Common. No house number, no street name, just plain Ash Common. And there are pages and pages of others sharing this same frugal address. The surnames reveal that this was a gypsy encampment and research confirms that one did exist for many years on Ash Common, with their descendants still living in and around that corner of Surrey today. Most of the inhabitants would have lived in a vardo – the ancestor of the modern caravan – or more likely bender tents, which were simple structures made from the branches of willow and hazel trees bent into a dome shape and covered with tarpaulins. It would have been a hard life.

I'd never have risked asking my grandmother, Minnie Chatt, about her swarthy, darker complexion and her possible Romany origins. Some sources on genealogical websites have Elijah as her stepfather, so she may not have been. I always assumed she had been permanently browned toiling in the sun-kissed hop fields of Kent as a child and a young woman. But now as I rifle my distant memory, I have this snippet of recall of one of my siblings whispering once that Gran's family were gypsies, with all the mystery and intrigue that entailed.

My mother – Vera Elizabeth Smith – came from a family that had some money. Once. Her father Charles, my grandfather, was a salesman and electrician in the 1901 census, and a hydraulic engineer by 1911. At the time he died in 1929 he was listed as living at the Glyn Arms public house in

Ewell on the road to Cheam, and I can remember family talk of him having owned a pub. The building is still there, although now it is a Toby Carvery where you can happily queue on a Sunday for half an hour for your roast beef, spuds and carrots. I often do.

Charles died of a heart attack after playing a game of tennis when he was in his early fifties. Significant to me, as a man who once had a keen interest in acquiring money, is that at the time of his death his assets were declared at £3,000. Doesn't sound a huge amount, but that three grand would be worth over £1 million at today's values. He left it mainly to his wife, my nan, but none of it filtered down to us. What happened to it? Where did it go? I'd love to know. Perhaps, if that dosh had still been sloshing around in the family, I'd never have chosen the career path that I did. Probably not, though.

My great-great-grandmother on my mother's side was a Susannah Gibbs, who married a geezer called William Balkwill, my great-great-grandfather. They lived in the small village of Huish in Devon. Susannah must have had something about her because in the 1880s she divorced William, not an easy or common thing for a woman to undertake in those days. Susannah alleged, and the divorce court agreed with her, that William was committing adultery on a regular basis with not one but two of the household servants. I don't know what shocks me more – the fact that my great-great-grandfather was a serial adulterer or the fact that we had two servants in the family.

My parents met in the Glyn Arms pub, coincidentally. William Field was returning from the Epsom Derby that had been run a couple of hours earlier just a few miles up the road. April the Fifth had won it that day in June 1932, ridden by jockey Fred Lane, uncle to Lester Piggott. Father may have had a few quid at 100/6 and was flush with the readies. Perhaps he turned Vera's head by buying her a drink and flashing the cash. Alternatively, she may have been in the pub and mentioned the family connection, and that turned his head. Who knows? However it happened, Vera and Bill were married the following year and had Pat soon after. I don't know at what point my mum discovered that my father was a habitual criminal.

Bill Field's villainous life was kept from me as a young child. I remember him in army uniform – I'm unsure if he was still wearing it after the war or I've just formed memories of him at that time from long-lost family photographs. He was a tall, good-looking man, and I was proud that he'd won a medal for his bravery in the bomb-disposal unit where he was taught how to deactivate enemy bombs. Regrettably, he transferred those skills into civilian life, where he used his explosives know-how for criminal ends. Bill became a good and sought-after safe blower. I remember being a bit crestfallen when it first dawned on me that my war-hero old man had become a cracksman.

Safe blowing as a line of work peaked in the 1950s and 60s. I guess there were plenty more wayward former soldiers who followed a similar career path to my father. Possibly the most famous peterman (another slang term for this 'profession') was E. W. Hornung's fictional Arthur J. Raffles, a gentleman thief who thought nothing of slipping out of the drawing room at an aristocratic cocktail party to blow the stately home safe with gelignite. In real life there was Scotsman Johnny Ramensky. He went in the opposite direction to my old man. He was a well-established peterman when the Second World War broke out, but he put his life of crime on hold and volunteered for the British Commandos, deploying and imparting his explosives savvy on several dangerous missions. Johnny resumed his illegal safe-blowing habit after the war and ended up being Scotland's most celebrated prison escapee, having broken out of Peterhead jail five times.

The most famous safecracker and big-time cat burglar – and a name I remember hearing about as a young man – was George 'Taters' Chatham. All sorts of unsubstantiated claims have been made about the millions he stole and the famous blags that he was on, but he certainly was prolific. His biggest claim to notoriety was managing to hoist the Duke of Wellington's ceremonial swords from the Victoria and Albert Museum. He served over thirty years in prison and died penniless, they say, in 1997. Some of you may also remember the 1963 British comedy film *The Cracksman*, where a hapless locksmith played by comedian Charlie Drake ends up getting tricked into blowing safes for a criminal gang. My old man was probably somewhere between old Taters and little Charlie Drake.

My father's most famous escapade that I know about was when he was part of a gang that robbed the famous Hawker aircraft factory in Kingston upon Thames, Surrey. He blew the safe open, the contents were hurriedly scooped out into holdalls and the team scarpered. When they reached the safe house and examined the proceeds of the robbery, they were alarmed to see that besides cash they'd taken some plans for the Hawker Harrier jump jet, which was then in development. The documents were stamped TOP SECRET. The old man realised that now not only would the Robbery Squad be on his tail, but mostly likely MI5 and Special Branch too. He didn't fancy getting hanged for treason or being permanently disappeared by the men in suits, so he somehow got the plans deposited discreetly at a local police station. If nothing else, my father was a patriot. Everyone was at the time.

The physical landscape when I was born was one scarred by the six-year-long Second World War that finally ended just a year before I arrived. Families bombed out of London tried to pick up the pieces, literally, on the new council estates that had been built to accommodate the migration away from the old London slum areas. Kids played among the debris of bombed-out buildings, their parents worked where they could find some, and tried to feed their families as best they could within the limitations of national food rationing and affordability. The war was the defining event for the generation above me. Most of those people talked in terms of 'before the war' and 'after the war' until the day they died. Now we say 'before Covid' and 'after Covid'.

The rumble of hunger in our tummies was an ever-present sensation in the 1940s, 50s and early 60s, but it wasn't until we began to eat properly as youths and adults that we realised it wasn't a natural one. Rationing finally ended in 1954, but not in our house. Us Fields were poor, even by the austere standards of the period. When asked about those days I tend to shrug and say, 'We knew no different.' By that I mean we experienced no different, so we couldn't *feel* what we were deprived of, but we could *see* different. We lived in Cheam in Surrey, for fuck's sake! Cheam, with its preserved, listed, timber-constructed medieval buildings, posh housing estates, manicured flower beds and charming little shops. Just down the road from us and stretching all the way down to Ewell was Nonsuch Park, where Henry VIII had once lived in the now-disappeared palace, and trotted around his grounds on a very strong horse, guzzling port and skewering deer. Next door was the esteemed Nonsuch Girls' School, a state school that thought it was private and punched above its weight.

Ironically, though, for the older generation, at least, Cheam was most famous for being the imaginary rented home of the deadpan radio and television comedian Tony Hancock, who resided at 23 Railway Cuttings, East Cheam, along with wide-boy cockney spiv Sid James. Us Fields also lived in rented accommodation, on Malden Road, Cheam, but there was precious little comedy or laughs to be had inside our house.

It wasn't a house of fun or a house of love, it was a house of horror underpinned by brutality, hopelessness and cruelty.

We shared the rooms with rats, mice and cockroaches. Why they came I do not know, as there were slim pickings to be had. My father left home when I was five, although due to the war he hadn't been around much before. He tended to come home on leave or between prison sentences, make Mum pregnant, then piss off again. That was the pattern by all accounts. When he finally disappeared for what we thought was for good, he left my mum with us kids at Malden Road with his parents – my grandmother Minnie Chatt and grandfather John Richard Field. John had fought in the Royal Artillery in the First World War and was a decent man. How he ended up with Gran, who as you'll read was a monster straight off the pages of a Charles Dickens novel, I'll never get my head around.

Grandfather died early in my life, so my memories of him are few and far between. My siblings who knew him better always said he was a lovely person. Unfortunately for all of us, with Grandfather now dead and my old man on the missing list, there was no brake on Minnie's evil behaviour. Her tyranny and cruelty went off the scale. And I haven't even got to Uncle Fred yet. He came to live with us after Grandfather and my father had gone.

Mum was in no position to protect us from Gran, or later, Uncle Fred. I sometimes heard Mum described as a broken woman. Her husband's drinking, playing around with other ladies, and going in and out of the nick was bad enough, but she also suffered terribly with elephantiasis and skin cancer. Probably depression too. That undiagnosed condition was called 'being a bit down' or 'not feeling quite myself' in those less understanding times. The elephantiasis manifested itself in one of her legs becoming enormous, like an elephant's leg, hence the shaming name. This rendered her immobile both physically and mentally, and I can still remember the rage and sorrow I felt as people in the street would stare openly and point at her sad, disfigured limb. Even as a young boy in short trousers I wanted to fly across the high street and lamp them.

I don't understand now why Mum's side of the family didn't help – there was money there, after all. I remember just once my Nan on the maternal side turning up at the house. In my head she was in a Rolls-Royce, but I guess it was just a posh car. She did certainly have a chauffeur, though, and she was wearing a fox fur, and when she left she took my little hand and wrapped it around a half-crown piece. The coin – heavy and silver – was worth two shillings and sixpence, 12.5p to you, but a small fortune to a young boy in the mid-50s. I had never clasped such riches. When Nan left, Gran looked hard at me, uncurled her hand and pointed to her palm. I had to hand it over. I'd been rich for all of five minutes. Mum looked at Gran with pleading eyes, but her eyes burned back. *She* was paying the bills was the message.

Mum would get National Assistance money from the government to help feed and clothe us kids, but Gran took it off her as soon as she collected it. Then she would give her back five bob, like she was doing her a favour. Pocket money for a grown woman. My poor mum had such a hard, humiliating life, and she too was as much at the mercy of that devil, Minnie Chatt, as we kids were. My hunch is that my grandparents were adamantly opposed to our parents marrying right from the get-go and took the attitude, you've made your own bed, now you must lie in it. Harsh, especially as Nan could clearly see the hardships we faced, even if she was unaware of the abuse.

I struggle to put into words how wicked my Gran was. A nasty piece of work. A beast, even. She tortured us all mentally and physically. Mum told me that when a German bomb landed in Lumley Road where the family had lived just before I was born, it blew the side of our house clean out. My brothers Ted and Billy, who were not much more than babies, were strapped into their beds in the attic and ended up in the garden. Thankfully, they were largely unhurt, but they were petrified and unable to move from their beds because Gran had tethered them to the frame. Mum said it was the fastest she saw Gran come out the cellar – where she was sheltering in the best place herself, of course – to get them unstrapped before the ARP wardens arrived and reported her cruelty.

I don't know to this day why Gran was so vicious to us. What happened to her that she routinely visited violence on little children? Maybe she resented having to put a roof over our heads and feed us. If anything, she should have been angry at her son, our old man, who had deserted us.

One day when Mum was in hospital, as she often was, Gran came in, sat down and called me over to her. I was about seven years old.

'Your mother's dead,' she stated without emotion.

'What?'

'Your mother just died in the hospital,' she repeated. She got up, patted down her apron and walked out of the room.

I couldn't see her face as she walked away, but I bet she was smiling. I was distraught, although I didn't cry aloud as Gran wouldn't have liked that. I went and stood in the corner, trying to contain my utter grief and fear. Later, one of my brothers told me it wasn't true, and that Mum was coming home. I didn't tell Mum what Gran had said. She would have denied it and paid me back worse. Why do a thing like that to a little boy? Taking pleasure from an infant's despair and terror can only be sadism. She was a bastard sadist.

2

DELIVER US FROM EVIL

Grandmother Minnie Chatt's abuse, as I now know to rightly call it, was sustained and severe. She'd whack you with her open hand or deliver a swift backhand, punch you with her fist and strike you with whatever household implement was close to hand. Her favourite offensive weapon, though, was her walking stick, which she hit my siblings with frequently. She preferred to use the knobbly end for maximum effect. Being sent flying across the room for some imagined misdemeanour was likely to happen whenever you were in her orbit.

Brother Ted, who was a quiet boy, had it the worst. He was well and truly brutalised. He had an allergy to cheese. Just couldn't eat the stuff as it made him retch, and Gran would stab it down his little throat with her diabolical fingers. Another time she poured scalding soup over his head because he wasn't eating it with the appreciation she demanded. He screamed in agony and jumped around the room like a demented creature. It really disturbed me. Fuck knows what mental as well as physical damage it did to Ted. I wanted to help this poor boy, but I was barely more than a toddler myself and was terrified of getting the same treatment. I saw both Peter and Ted knocked out cold with that damned stick of hers. I was lucky that my brothers absorbed most of the violence that could have come my way, but as I got older I was battered too. I had no reason to believe that this didn't happen in all homes.

Like most of my siblings at various times, Ted was put into care at a children's home in Redhill when there wasn't enough money to feed us all, or so Gran told us. I believe I was the only one of the children not to spend any time in care. Knowing what we know now about what took place in many of those institutions, I wonder what further indignities and horrors Ted withstood in there, but I feel and desperately hope it was a welcome respite from living with Gran. I think, given the choice and if we could have stayed together, we'd have all opted for going into care. That's how desperate our situation was.

As soon as he could, Ted fled Malden Road, joined the army and served in Cyprus. He was driving an officer around in a jeep one day when a petrol bomb was thrown into his lap and exploded, and he was terribly burned. He spent a lot of time in rehabilitation in Aldershot, and I was taken by my sisters Pat and Cissy to see him in a military hospital. He had written earlier and said that he'd made me a model of a jousting medieval knight. When we got to the hospital it was hard to tell people apart as they were all bandaged so heavily. I

28

yelped excitedly, 'There he is!' and pointed. Pat asked how I could be sure. I'd seen the model knight on a horse with a jousting stick on his bedside table.

Billy also had it bad from Gran and he too got put into a home. Sometimes he came back for a while, then he was gone again. He was a good boy. When he started work as a cable joiner he brought money into the house regularly to ease our poverty, and he continued to support us even after he'd found a flat to live in.

I shared a bedroom with my mum, sleeping on the hard floor with some blankets and a pillow. The others slept all together in another bedroom, and Gran had a bedroom to herself. She'd also designated the front room facing the road as her space only. Mum wasn't even allowed in, and unlike the rest of the house it was kept spotless and pristine. I never knew what that was all about. I wonder now if Gran entertained men. It wouldn't surprise me, as I was told once that during the First World War she'd been a brass. No joking, I think I'd rather have served more time on the front line than get close up and personal with her.

My sisters Pat and Cissy were the light in our darkness, providing some of the love and warmth Mum was unable to fully give, and that Gran, who simply didn't have love in her, refused to. Pat got out the house too as soon as possible when she married Johnny at just seventeen, but she still came and fetched me out of what I now recognise was a waking nightmare when she could. I remember Pat and Johnny taking me to a show that was put on by the Post Office one Christmas.

Pat must have worked there. They gave me a Post Office set with a little cash register that went ding and working miniature scales to go home with. After Pat went, Cissy took over as the maternal sibling. She wasn't strong enough to stop the beatings dished out by Gran – and later, Uncle Fred – but she helped keep us out of their way and was a calming, soft female presence in the home.

Christmas was little different from any other time of the year for us. Dire. We had no turkey, no decorations, no cards, no presents. It brought home how we lived in comparison with others. I'd walk past neighbouring houses and see wreaths on the doors, the front rooms lit up and promising warmth, a flickering tinsel-covered Christmas tree, children excited and chattering, black and white televisions glowing in the corner. It was a million miles from life in our house. If carol singers made the mistake of turning up on our doorstep, I'd be wondering how much money they had in their collection box and how I could pinch it.

We did eventually get a television set when Billy began bringing money into the house. God bless him, that first television was six inches – the size of a small biscuit tin – and we set up a giant magnifying glass in front of it so we could actually see the picture. The lens was filled with water for some reason. It was like watching the picture through a goldfish bowl, but it was better than not watching at all. These contraptions were not rare at the time.

Cissy started courting a barrow boy from Tooting Market called Tony. He was a decent bloke and made more difference to our lives than he probably realised. From the market he came bearing gifts: oranges and apples, carrots and potatoes, and even underwear, an exotic luxury in the Field household. It was a living shame for us boys and we were constantly in fear of being exposed, literally. Tony always brought home a packet of Weights non-tipped cigarettes for Mum. He bought me Airfix models that I'd carefully construct with glue, and then paint. I remember a Spitfire plane that was my pride and joy.

Gran, typically, showed no gratitude, and one afternoon hit Tony on the swede with a milk bottle. Why, I do not know. The bottle didn't smash but cut Tony's forehead. He stood up and poured the milk from a jug over Gran's head, which delighted us all, although we couldn't show it. Gran's violence was always there, bubbling away, battling to escape. Sometimes she'd boil over and go into the Prince of Wales pub almost next door to pick a fight with a man or a woman – or both. These days she'd be sectioned.

The food that Tony produced was a godsend, as we'd been practically starved by Gran. All our neighbours could see. There wasn't an ounce of fat between all us kids. Grandfather had educated me on mushrooms, which ones were safe to eat and which weren't. Mushrooms didn't survive long in Nonsuch Park. Normal families picnicking in the park must have seen us stuffing them down our throats like demented feral children and shaken their heads in pity.

Bill White next door ran the (then) illegal bookies – even today there's a sign on the front of the house saying 'The

Old Bookmakers' – and Nanny White, his wife, would secretly pass sandwiches and apples over the fence to us. What a compassionate woman she was. I'd stand in the garden with my back to the house and wolf the sarney down without barely moving so Gran wouldn't realise we were being fed. We didn't dare ask for food. On one occasion when Peter did raise the possibility of having something to eat, she made him drink Friars' Balsam, which tasted vile I imagine, and had the effect of making him dizzy like he was drunk. I can picture the fucking witch now, sitting in her chair, smoking a long clay pipe, or maybe a cigar, like a satanic Popeye, relishing Peter's distress and confusion, the offending walking stick leaning up against her chair ominously.

Nanny White would also sometimes give me money for doing her shopping, which if I could get away with it I'd spend at Saturday morning pictures at the Century picture house. Watching Flash Gordon, Laurel and Hardy, Roy Rogers and Trigger, Hopalong Cassidy and Old Mother Riley was a delightful couple of hours' escape from the sordid life in Malden Road. I was particularly attracted to Jesse James, who robbed banks but was clearly a hero, drawing cheers from the kids when he shot himself free from pursuing sheriffs and marshals. This was my earliest exposure to armed robbery. Did it enter my subconscious that no person – child or adult – leaving those cinemas ever muttered, 'Tut, tut, tut, those James brothers were bad men holding up all those banks and trains'?

No, they were icons to us. Yes, the outlaws were officially the baddies – and the sheriffs the goodies – but I'll wager that when young boys played cowboys, as they did in my childhood, few of them ever imagined they were the sheriff, and the majority were Jesse or his brother Frank.

Auntie Mary and Uncle Jim were also truly kind. They weren't real blood relations – you could end up being called an uncle or an auntie if you delivered the paraffin in those days – but their garden backed onto ours. They also smuggled us food and kept an eye on us. I don't think there were any social services to report us to in those days. Mary and Jim and Nanny White knew that to openly show us charity or express concern about our well-being would only result in more pain and punishment for us kids. They walked a tightrope. It was a desperate situation but common, I suspect.

We'd get around the back of the greengrocer's shop down the road and have away what produce was lying around. We nicked the baker's loaves from behind that shop and anything else we thought could be eaten. Directly next door to us was the Sale Room – an auction house – and we'd sneak in behind there and sort through the junk that hadn't sold, then take it home. They probably knew, and saw it as saving them the chore of getting rid. What we didn't cart off they'd burn. Sometimes I'd take home an old flea-bitten mattress on my back, or grey coarse army-issue blankets. There were always unwanted worn-out shoes piled up, and Gran never told us off for this pilfering. The shoes invariably went on the fire for heat.

Years later the author Kate Kray took me back there to the Sale Room and our old house next door for a television documentary, and I think she had half a mind to knock on the door of my childhood home and take us inside. I suddenly felt rising panic. I could not and would not enter that miserable and painful house again. Kate tried to draw me out on my bad memories, but I kept them locked up. This is the first time I've gone into any detail about what went on in Malden Road, seventy years later, not only because it's painful to remember but because of all the shame I've been holding onto. It wasn't my fault, but I feel shame, nevertheless.

Across the road from us was a scouts' hut where jumble and bring-and-buy sales were regularly held. For those of you under the age of fifty, jumble sales were the forerunner of car-boot sales, except they were usually held for charitable purposes not individual profit. Boy scouts would knock on prosperous residential doors in the days before the sale asking for 'any jumble'. Us Fields would watch and wait across the road like desperate scavengers for the proceedings to finish, then we'd scurry over and rifle the tables and cardboard boxes for anything left that we could use or burn. Mum had an eye for something of better quality, perhaps an unwanted or broken toy. I remember a little wind-up clockwork train that she put by for a rare Christmas present. We never had shop-bought gifts. The organisers would watch us with pity, but they wouldn't intervene as they were good, caring people – and also, we saved them the ache of getting rid of the unwanted, unsaleable junk.

Uncle Fred, my father's brother, came to live with us, although I was never sure why. He worked as a coalman, and he paid Gran board and lodgings. He hadn't served in the army – I was never sure why of that either. He was a big man with a strong upper body formed through humping heavy bags of coal around. I don't imagine coalmen qualified as a reserved occupation, yet somehow he'd swerved that call-up. He soon had me up the coal yard at four in the morning, barely awake, crusty sleep almost sealing my eyes, helping load and unload the coal sacks. I went to school later on, not only dog tired but with soot and coal dust ingrained in my skin. It did mean that I got a whole desk to myself, as nobody would want to sit next to me. It goes without saying that Fred never paid me for my labour.

It wasn't long before Uncle Fred started striking us too. Not as frequently as Gran did, but you knew it when you got a clump off him. Normally it would be when he got in from the Prince of Wales. He'd be rocking backward and forward pissed and ask a question, then belt us for 'answering back'. If you did something wrong – I can't think what – he had a big old belt like one you'd strap around a horse's belly and he'd hit us with that. When he delivered a punch it was like he was up against the village prize fighter; he took no account of the fact that we were children. I'm surprised nobody was killed. He was an absolute bastard, and when he showed up, life became even worse – if that was possible. I'd like to know what Gran charged Fred for his bed and board, and a licence to beat her defenceless little grandchildren and his nephews on demand.

When I was twelve, maybe thirteen, I started to harbour violent thoughts and impulses. They were mainly directed at Gran and Uncle Fred, and various boys and teachers at school. I was developing a diabolical temper, and – shamefully – I even took out my rage on Cissy and my brothers. I was turning very quickly into a vicious, nasty little bastard.

One day it all boiled over. It was a massive turning point in my life. I heard Mum crying out in the hallway, and I ran there to see Gran hitting her with the fucking stick and my sick mother shielding her head to ward off the blows. Gran was screaming something about her not having cleaned the stairs. I leapt at Gran and got my hands around her wretched neck. The blood pumped around my body, and I squeezed and squeezed like my life depended on it. I felt great. Empowered. Gran's eyes bulged, and she started to turn blue and was making choking noises, which was understandable as I was choking her.

I could hear Mum sobbing and shouting at me to stop and let her go, but I wanted to finish the job. If I could kill her, the pain would go for all of us. If I went to borstal, it surely couldn't be worse than this existence in Malden Road. I gave no thought to the consequences. Gran was sinking to her knees, and Mum grabbed my hands and tried to loosen my stranglehold, prising my fingers away. I suddenly came out of my rage, let her go and drop to the floor, dribbling, coughing and spluttering, and walked into another room. Gran never said a word about the incident – and neither did Mum – but she never struck me or her again.

Brother Billy was of an age now where Gran and Uncle Fred couldn't hit him anymore, and now the violence had subsided we could all see just how bad it was. My inner rage swirled around my head. I now knew that other families were *not* like ours, that the conditions we lived in and the brutality we endured were *not* normal and were wrong. Very wrong.

Billy and I started to talk about it one day, and my brother casually remarked, 'You know Uncle Fred raped Pat, don't you?'

'He did what? When?'

'I don't know when, it happened more than once.'

'What about Cissy?'

'I don't know about Cissy. I hope not.'

It took me a while to process the revelation, and I wondered if the shitbag had ever tried it on with Mum or even one of my brothers. I was old enough and sufficiently streetwise to appreciate the horror of rape and the damage it's likely to cause. I went to bed that night seething and forming a plan in my head to kill my uncle. That information from Billy changed my life.

The next night was a weekend, and I knew that Fred would be in the Prince of Wales until chucking-out time around 10.30 p.m. I selected a heavy concrete brick from the garden and went to the bathroom window upstairs that looked down over the back door that Fred would come stumbling to any minute. The drunken pig approached, swaying from side to side and mumbling to himself, and I lashed the brick down on his fat head with more force than I'd ever mustered in my life, and he went down like a sack of spuds. A bag of fucking coal. I leapt down the stairs, burst out the back door and kicked the shit out of him before he could recover and react. I stamped and jumped on his head and body like a wild animal. If I'd had a knife, I've no doubt I'd have cut his poxy throat.

'That's for Pat,' I screamed.

'I never done it,' he moaned.

Never done what? How did he know what I was talking about? Gran heard the commotion, and came out and asked me calmly to stop. She even said please. She looked at Uncle Fred lying there gurgling in a puddle of dark red blood, but never asked why. She knew. She went down the road to the phone box and called for an ambulance. I went up to bed and slept like a baby.

3

HEY, KID, LEAVE THOSE TEACHERS ALONE

Uncle Fred never came back to live at Malden Road. He knew if he did, I'd murder him. There was no doubt. He wasn't going to go to the police either, was he? Fred packed up and left. He later married the girl that once ran a jellied eel stall with my mum that set up at the weekends outside the Red Lion pub in Cheam. I saw him only once more in his scummy life, and that was when he turned up for a funeral about a decade later. He offered to buy me a drink. Fuck off, I said. I did turn up to his funeral, though. I waited for the few mourners that were there to drift off and I pissed on his grave.

The family dynamic had changed for ever. I was no longer scared of Gran or Fred. I was growing bigger and stronger fast. I was not scared of anyone, truth be told, child or adult. And I'd certainly not allow anyone to bully, abuse, mock or knock me about ever again. And even if they were bigger, better or stronger than me, I'd tip the odds in my favour by whatever means necessary. It was an ethos that I've stuck to throughout my life. I enjoyed the violence I'd unleashed on Gran and Fred, and was looking for an opportunity to do it again. Revenge and rage were in my heart. I was turning into a bloody menace.

I was technically still at school but I was calling the shots at home, although there weren't many shots to call. There was no more brutality in the house, and Peter, Billy and I were the only kids left. Gran's health was poor. Mum's health was poor. And then without any announcement or warning, my father came back. It was the early 1960s, and Billy came in one late afternoon and said casually, 'Dad's in the pub.' He didn't seem too pleased. My curiosity aroused, I went into the Prince of Wales to see for myself.

'Hello, stranger,' he winked, as he tipped a pint of mild down his throat.

I was pleased to see him. I understood that he lived on the wrong side of the law, but I wasn't bothered about that. I secretly admired villainy by now. However, I didn't know then he had knocked our mum about. If I had, things would have been different. It was this knowledge, I guess, that explains why Billy, Peter and Mum weren't too happy about his sudden reappearance. Mum had hinted to me about the domestic violence she'd suffered from the old man, although she was never specific, but I didn't want to consider it and parked what she'd said in the back of my mind. Dad breezed back into our lives as if he'd never been away. The prodigal husband. He had more front than Eastbourne.

Dad got me working. Instead of going to school, I started renovating some houses down in Brighton. One early evening I returned home. Mum looked concerned.

'Gran has died,' she said softly.

'Good,' I replied.

She didn't say what she'd died of, and I didn't ask. I just hoped there was plenty of suffering.

I should have been in school, but my attendance had always been intermittent. I didn't mind school like some; it was better than being at home much of the time, but it was clear I was different from the other kids. I had a friend then who lived nearby called Susan, whose old man had also gone on the missing list. Other kids teased us, saying my old man was a 'jailbird' and her dad was a 'runaway'. To me they added that I was dirty and smelly. They were right. We rarely got a decent wash at home, let alone a bath.

Our difference from other teenagers was underlined when sister Dalla was brought to see us by her adoptive parents. That was not very often, despite her living less than a mile away in one of the grand houses in South Cheam with their sweeping in-and-out driveways and tall hedges. When she came she looked a picture in her posh coat and bonnet, and although Dalla was our sister, she was like an alien turning up at the house. Two different worlds. At least her adoptive parents felt that it was right that she shouldn't lose complete touch with her birth family.

I first started school at Chatsworth Road Infants, then Malden Road Juniors and finally Chatsworth Road Seniors, which I understand is now referred to as Cheam High. Mr Gilbert was the headmaster at the juniors. The kids nicknamed him Gobby Gilbert, but he was a fair man. At the senior school the head was an ex-RAF pilot, Mr Hall. I didn't cross his path much.

David Bellamy, the bearded and lisping naturalist from 1970s television who disappeared from our screens when he declared that global warming was a hoax, went to Malden Road Juniors a few years before me. In one newspaper article he recalled:

> I moved to the big boys' school. If you got your tables wrong too many times, our teacher Mrs Gray would force you to stand beside her desk facing the class with your head in a net bag used for carrying footballs. After her, I moved to Mr Hedges' class. He was the ultra-fit games master who whacked you with a ruler or threw the board duster with perfect aim. Then it was Mr Jamieson who, in winter, tended a cauldron over a coal fire in the classroom, where he cooked soup that could be bought for lunch for a penny.

In that paragraph David captures school life as it was then. Teachers were sometimes violent, sometimes eccentric, and nobody thought anything of it. Only now does the brutality of hulking great men striking little children with long sticks shock. Imagine it happening outside the school environment; even then, say in Nonsuch Park, the police would have been called, and nowadays the teacher would get nicked. It was a hangover from Victorian times that endured long past its sell-by date.

One subject I did enjoy at school was reading, even though I didn't manage to write to any decent standard until much later. I liked books, and one author in particular helped me through my miserable childhood: Enid Blyton. Bless her soul. At school they had her *Famous Five* and *Secret Seven* books, and I lost myself in a world of balmy summer days, bottles of pop, boys and girls on bikes charging around the countryside with Timmy the mongrel dog yapping alongside them, foiling criminals and dastardly plots. When I was reading I was somewhere else other than Malden Road and in the vicinity of the wrath of Gran and Uncle Fred. One day I asked the teacher if I could take one of the books home from school. Of course, she said, but you must bring it back. The next day I handed it in to her.

'Didn't you like it, Ronnie?'

'Yes, it was brilliant.'

'You read it in one evening?'

'Yes.'

She looked at me over her glasses as teachers did when they thought you were fibbing but didn't want to call you a liar.

'Can I take another?'

I took the next one home and returned it the following morning.

'Are you really reading these, Ronnie?' asked the teacher doubtfully.

'Yes, ask me any question about it.'

She flicked open the book and asked me who George the tomboy was sitting next to on the coach or some such question. Julian, I answered. The teacher was impressed, and I worked my way through the next thirty books. I hear that these days Enid Blyton is accused of racism, sexism and writing not very good children's literature. Well, I and millions of kids loved them, and for some children she was a vital light in their dark lives. From Enid I moved on to Sherlock Holmes, which was harder to read but worth the effort. Elementary, my dear Field. I also read the Biggles books by Captain W. E. Johns and anything else I could lay my hands on.

I now had some close pals: Terry Hobson, Ginger Bob Skinner and Trevor Booth were the main ones, and we flirted with the fading Teddy Boy culture. Trevor joined the army when he left school and for a while I contemplated following him. I could have been firing a gun with Her Majesty's approval. Most boys thought Trev was mad for enlisting and me for even considering it, as our age group had dodged being called up for National Service by the skin of our teeth, the compulsory call-up having only being abolished a year or two earlier. I wonder how different my life would have been had I had been conscripted to the army.

There was another friend who I sat next to who'd contracted polio and had to wear callipers on his legs. Polio was a disease that by the 1960s had been mainly eliminated, although evidence of it lingered on. It didn't stop him trying to look like a Teddy Boy. The Teds were the first widespread youth cult over here, first coming to public attention in the early 1950s. They were into rock 'n' roll music, greased-back hair called a 'Duck's Arse', drape suits and winklepicker or crepe shoes, and they outraged society by fighting each other in gangs and slashing cinema seats with flick knives. There was a tragic incident on Clapham Common that dominated the news for a while when two groups of Teds had clashed and one boy, John Beckley, was stabbed and killed. Michael Davies, a member of the so-called Plough Boys gang, named after a pub on Clapham High Street, was charged with murder and then faced being hanged, but was reprieved from the condemned cell at the last minute. It was widely thought that Davies had been set up, and it doesn't surprise me to read that one of the young coppers on the case was Kenneth Drury. More on that bent policeman later.

Nearer to home, and something I remember more clearly, was the case of Christopher Craig and Derek Bentley, which filled the newspapers for months. The sad fate of Bentley was a talking point for years. They were two friends – Craig was sixteen and Bentley nineteen – who screwed a sweet manufacturing factory in Tamworth Road, Croydon, and ended up having a shootout with the police. Or, at least, the boy Craig did. Bentley, who was educationally backward, was unarmed and passive under police arrest. PC Sidney Miles was shot dead before Craig was finally apprehended on the factory roof. Both boys were found guilty of murder, with Bentley sentenced to hang due to his age and being an accessory to the killing, while Craig was judged too young to be executed, even though he'd fired the gun. Unlike Michael Davies before him, poor old Derek was not reprieved, and he was strung up and strangled by hangman Albert Pierrepoint. Bentley's family fought for many years to clear his name, and in the 1990s he finally received a royal pardon. A bit too late for the unfortunate lad. Christopher Craig served a ten and was out, never to darken a police station door again, as far as I know.

Craig's older brother Niven was a well-known criminal in south London and an armed robber. He blamed himself for what happened on the Croydon rooftop because his kid brother hero-worshipped him and his outlaw ways. In 1961, however, it was Niven who was in the headlines, not Christopher, when he was one of ten men who sensationally broke out of Wandsworth Prison. Questions about Niven's case were raised in Parliament.

Of course, I never had all the Ted gear but I did my best. I remember liking Joe Brown and getting the money together to buy his single, 'A Picture of You'. It was the first record I ever purchased once Billy fetched a gramophone into the house. I liked Joe as he seemed like one of the boys, unlike Cliff Richard and his backing group, the robotic Shadows. Earlier I'd been aware of the film *Blackboard Jungle* causing a stir, and the massive popularity of the song 'Rock Around the Clock' by Bill Haley and the Comets, which featured in the film. This movie, that song and the Teddy Boy youth cult spurred a moral panic over teenagers and so-called juvenile delinquents. Most boys of my age and background wanted to be a train driver when they grew up or a pilot or even a policeman. Not me. I wanted to be a Ted and a juvenile delinquent.

I never slashed a cinema seat and I mainly avoided trouble at school. One boy and I fell out over him calling me dirty or smelly, or both. I'd had enough of all this now and was answering back. I forget his name, so let's call him John. Well, when I said at least I haven't got a big fucking nose, John challenged me to a fight and I had no choice but to agree. He beat me fair and square, and I went home battered, bloody and bruised but not massively bothered. I'd already decided that in future I wouldn't allow my physical inferiority in a one-to-one to handicap me, and was biding my time.

I spotted John a few years later when we both ventured into the adult working world and were spending our pay packets in the Red Lion pub in Cheam. I popped back home and fetched a baseball bat, and leant it up against the wall. I went back in and offered him outside.

'Remember me, doncha?' I said.

'There's no need for this,' he responded, nervously eyeing what I was reaching for outside the door.

'There is,' I said, and I promptly pummelled him senseless with the bat.

There were two other boys in my class that goaded me more than most. Gerald and David were their names, and they were identical twins. Their poor treatment of me was never physical, as that wasn't their game. Gerald and David came from money, always well dressed and manicured, hair Brylcreemed back, with nice Claud Butler bikes and pressed and ironed school uniforms. They probably lived in the posh end of Cheam, with Daddy working in the City and boarding the train to Victoria station every morning. The twins teased me about my hand-me-down clothing and would pinch their noses when in my vicinity, as if offended by my body odour. Deodorant was as rare as caviar in our family house. They claimed I 'ponged'. It was cruel, and I learned not to react and to pretend I hadn't noticed their antics or heard their comments.

Two teachers stick in my mind. The first – I can't remember his name, but we made his life a misery. He clearly couldn't control the boys and wasn't cut out for the job. One day I was part of a pack of pupils that tied him up, lifted the vaulting horse, trapped him under it and left him there. We could hear him panicking and banging inside. I'm not saying the two events are connected, but weeks later the school announced sombrely he wouldn't be coming back as he'd committed suicide. He hanged himself. I didn't feel guilty for my small part in his demise. I should have, but I didn't.

The other master I recall was Mr Witley, a geography teacher, yet another bullying adult sadist I encountered in my childhood. Witley was famous for nailing a plimsoll onto the end of an eighteen-inch broom handle and leaving the weapon on prominent display in the classroom. That would have been acceptable had this bizarre implement just been a deterrent and a bit of fun, but it wasn't. Witley used it frequently on the boys, including me, for stupid reasons. Farting, fidgeting, yawning. He seemed to find it hilarious to slipper a boy on the arse from halfway across the classroom. What was wrong with these people? Had the war turned them into beasts? Who policed their behaviour? Of course, I didn't tell Gran I was being hit with this broom handle/plimsoll combo, not wanting to give her ideas.

One cold December evening I saw Witley as I was loitering without intent near my house. He was attending a carol service in nearby St Dunstan's Church, so I nipped indoors and got my trusty bat. I think it was the first time I wore a balaclava for nefarious purposes. I waited behind a tree after the service ended, and as he walked past in the graveyard I stepped out and smacked him across the nut. Take that, you fucking bully! I gave him a couple of whacks on the arse too, so hopefully he'd get the message. I left him there on the path and went indoors to watch *Rawhide* on the floaty television set.

4

NO ORDINARY JOE

When I was fourteen the fair came to Cheam and I was mesmerised. The bumper cars. The thrilling rides. The candy floss. The hot dogs. The girls. The Buddy Holly music blaring out. The smell of deep-fried chips mixed with engine oil. The film *That'll Be the Day* with David Essex, Ringo Starr and Billy Fury years later captured it perfectly. I was in my element, and when fairground men Bobby and Nosher Smith invited me to travel with them, I quickly agreed.

We went first to Epsom Downs and then all around the south of England, where I was manning the coconut shy, the darts and the hoopla. It was an apprenticeship. Bobby searched me at first, making sure I wasn't pilfering any of the takings, but he soon learned I had no wish to have him over. It was enough for me to be immersed in the fairground life, being on the open road and sleeping in a trailer. I watched the older boys working the dodgems and admired their skill in deftly swerving the cars, swinging around the poles and dropping change into the open palms of wide-eyed pretty giggling girls. My mum and Gran didn't raise any objection when I first said I was travelling with the fair for a few days. I was gone six months. Nobody alerted the police. I'm glad they didn't. It was like I'd found a family where the adults treated me with respect and decency. I savoured every minute. Up to that point it was the best period of my life.

Often fights would break out. The local tough nuts didn't like the fairground boys coming on their manor and would set about one or two of us when they thought the numbers were in their favour. They didn't appreciate the way their girls seemed besotted by the dodgem boys, particularly. The fair boys were greasy, tough, rough and ready, but it doesn't matter how tough you are if the numbers are against you. However, a shout would go up, and strong men and boys would appear from all over the site and deal decisively with the town boys. I lapped it up.

Old Mrs Smith, Bobby's mother, took me inside her caravan one day. I'd never seen such luxury. Such opulence. Beautiful lace curtains, soft crushed-velvet settees and chairs, Crown Derby china all over the show – I was scared to move in case I knocked anything over. I now knew how an ornament felt. She took my palm in her hand and traced her finger lightly over it. She was smiling at first, but then began to frown. I looked down at my palm to see if I could see what was disturbing her.

'Oh, Ronnie. I don't see good things. I see trouble ahead. I don't think you'll come to any good. Please be careful.'

Mrs Smith folded my hand and passed it back to me.

'Thanks, Mrs Smith.'

I wish she'd kept that one from me. Sometimes honesty is not the best policy. Why didn't she make up some lies about me finding a beautiful wife, having five healthy children, winning the 'Spot the Ball' competition in the newspaper and living happy ever after? I started to think more bad things were going to happen to me in life and there was fuck-all I could do about it. My life was mapped out. Why be good, why behave, if at the end of the day I'm going to come to no good? Mrs Smith said so and she can see the future.

On my return from my fairground tour of the Home Counties, Mum told me that the school-board man had been around and they were now about to take legal action against her about my non-attendance. I reluctantly said goodbye to my new fairground family and returned to Chatsworth Road School. Mr Hall, the headmaster, said you can't come into school like that. Like what? He was concerned I had no semblance of a uniform, that I was dressed like a Ted, and my hair was too long and greased back. Dodgem style. He kindly gave me a tanner for a haircut, but there was no way they were going to finance a uniform. The school-board man was also a fair chap. He used to come into the house to talk about my truancy and lack of engagement, but he could see our situation was a desperate one. One of my lasting memories of regular school is being sent home because of the Cuban Missile Crisis. I guess they were sending us back to our families to prepare for the end of the world. Strange times.

It all became academic anyway because soon there were no parents to take to court. My father was up to his old tricks again and hadn't paid any rent since Gran died, and we were eventually evicted. My parents moved to Fulham, Billy got a flat and Peter took lodgings somewhere. Quicker than you can tear up a summons letter, the little house by the dairy was no more. Malden Road was over, and the Fields had flown.

I visited my parents at their basement flat in Fulham, and it was a worse situation for my mum. Her elephantiasis and skin cancer were still present, and she had to drag herself up two flights of stairs of this large, old Victorian house to use the bathroom. The flat was cramped, damp and a dump, and I assume my father was still not treating her well. Mum's life, unfortunately, remained an unhappy one.

My first legitimate job was for a builder in Worcester Park. I was labouring, assisting the bricklayer, and earned two pounds and ten shillings a week. I really enjoyed it as it was mainly small extension jobs, and besides knocking muck up and carting bricks around I was able to try my hand at brick-laying. I liked working with my hands.

Later, for more money, I moved to Pennell Tree Fellers, work I also enjoyed. I knew a bit about the game as my father had lopped trees during his erratic runs of lawful employment. He was good at it, and I remember as a young kid when he had the task of bringing down the biggest tree in Cheam Park. He boasted to his colleagues and some random people in the park exactly where he'd land it. A small crowd gathered. He even took a couple of bets, and to add to the drama got me to stand still in the area just beyond where he estimated the tree would fall. Now I knew how the boy with the apple on his bonce in 'William Tell' felt. It's hard to believe that unknown men placed bets that meant they were hoping a nine-year-old boy would be grimly crushed to death in order to win a few shillings. I'll never forget the wind on my face as the monster tree sailed downward through the air and landed just a few feet in front of me. It blew me over. As I picked myself up I saw Dad with his hands on his hips, rocking backwards and laughing his head off.

I then got a job with Peter Ransome, who had a local gardening business where I worked as a fencer, turfer and general labourer for a few years. Peter's niece was a pretty girl called Carol and I liked her straight away. She must have felt the same way because her mother knocked on my door and asked if her daughter could come to my sixteenth birthday party at the house. With Gran gone, this was a short period when we could do what we wanted at home. I put my best Teddy Boy gear on – my wardrobe was expanding now I had money in my pocket – collected Carol from her house opposite the Jenny Lind pub in Sutton and took her back to my own party.

When I knocked on the door her stepdad answered and called out behind him, 'Carol, there's something at the door for you.'

Something? I'll always remember that. I hope he was joking.

The next day Carol came around again and suggested we 'go out' together. I said yes, and that was it. We were now courting, as they used to say. Because my home framework had disintegrated, I shortly moved in with Carol and her parents, who were kind to take me, and then I moved nearby to lodge with a friend of Carol's parents. In digs, they called it then.

I was visiting pubs regularly by the age of sixteen and seventeen. I can remember being in another Red Lion – the one in Sutton – and I could hear the band playing. The music was loud, urgent and demanding. I normally didn't take much interest in so-called pop music, but these scruffy, long-haired boys were good, an antidote to the squeaky-clean, mop-topped, suited Beatles everybody was raving about. Teenagers in polo-neck jumpers were nodding their heads vigorously to the beat. The lead singer leapt around the stage, pouting his lips and thrusting out his backside.

'Who's this lot?' I asked my mate.

'Call themselves the Rolling Stones,' he replied.

Coincidentally I knew their publicist Les Perrin's son, who was local. What happened to them, I wonder?

With my mates Terry, Ginger Bob, Trevor and others we were getting a bit busy around the pubs of Sutton and Cheam, and were known not to shy away from a row. Also, some of us were thieving, supplementing our wages with pinching and selling copper – things like that. At the same time we got to know of some of the top 'faces' around town. The most famous of these was Joey Pyle. He was talked about in hushed tones when he entered the pub you were in with his fearsome-looking entourage in tow. He had an aura about him, but you dare not look over for too long. A solid man, having been a professional boxer, he was impeccably dressed in Savile Row tailored suits and shirts, and he always wore a tie. In the winter he had a luxurious Crombie coat complete with velvet collar. I never saw Joe not in a sharp suit until the latter days, when he developed a penchant for loose-fitting Hawaiian shirts. He looked the business. Always. Even before I spoke to him, I admired him.

When I saw him for the first time in the Red Lion, my chum Dave Challis nodded over and said, 'See that bloke over there. That's Joey Pyle, that is.'

I'd already clocked him arrive and knew instinctively who he was. Not many people dressed as well as Joe on the manor.

Joe had been in the national news just a few years earlier when he stood trial with Jimmy Nash and John Read at the Old Bailey for the murder of Selwyn Cooney, a London businessman who operated the New Cabinet Club in Gerrard Street. Cooney was shot dead inside the Pen Club at Spitalfields in the early hours of a Sunday morning during a fight over some money that was owed, although some said the reason was gangland friction. Another man was shot but not killed. The trial was stopped after it was alleged that jurors had been 'approached' and a barmaid witness made herself scarce. Other witnesses had also dropped out of the legal process. At the second trial the prosecution offered no evidence against Joe and John, and Jimmy Nash was eventually acquitted of murder due to lack of evidence. All three were later sentenced to prison on lesser charges.

Joe, when asked about who murdered Cooney, would often say to the press that Cooney must have walked past a passing bullet. The three of them had spent several weeks in custody when the murder rap was hanging over them and must have fretted over the real possibility of facing the hangman.

We were still merrily executing criminals then. Only a few months later Francis Forsyth was hanged in Wandsworth Prison following his guilty verdict for the senseless murder of man on a footpath in Hounslow. His mate Norman Harris, who was also in on the unprovoked attack, swung with him. Another friend of Forsyth, Victor Terry, heard about the double execution on his car radio and an hour later shot dead a security guard in the course of an armed robbery in Worthing. At his trial he claimed to be possessed by the spirit of the American gangster Legs Diamond. That didn't go down well, and in May 1961 Terry was hanged on the same gallows as Forsyth and Harris.

Joe told me once that when in custody awaiting trial, him and Jimmy Nash exchanged jokes about being executed. Black humour may have been the only way to deal with their predicament. When Joe opened up the boxing magazine *The Ring* in his cell, which had been read by Jimmy first, a shoelace tied as a noose would drop out. Also, on exercise Jimmy would stretch his neck in exaggerated head-turning moves and encouraged Joe to do the same. The screws thought they were mad.

'What are you two doing?' enquired a warder.

'We're strengthening our neck muscles so we can beat that blasted noose,' replied Jimmy.

The press saw the collapse of the Cooney trial as growing proof that the criminal 'underworld' in London was becoming stronger and more organised. The FBI may have been the Untouchables in America, but over here, the media reckoned, it was London's criminals and gangsters that the authorities couldn't lay a finger on. It was a theme they'd develop over the decade because it sold papers. Soon the hysteria they stirred up and encouraged was turbo-charged by the Great Train Robbery, and it would reach a feverish climax when the two leading London criminal firms – the Krays and the Richardsons – were brought down towards the end of the 1960s.

Down in Cheam, back in the early 60s, we'd heard of top gangsters Billy Hill, Jack Spot and the Nash family from Islington, and those young East End brothers called Kray were being talked about more and more and popping up in our newspapers, but Joey Pyle was very real and very much on our manor.

One day in the Red Lion Joe sent me over a drink and I nodded over my thanks. We'd never spoken, and I wasn't aware he knew who I was. I was flattered and a bit nervous, but didn't want to seem overkeen or overawed. Next time I went to the bar I offered him a drink back. We chatted and I immediately warmed to him. He smiled a great deal and had a strong charisma that stayed with him until his dying day. Everyone wanted to say hello to him, and he was always polite back to everyone, no matter who they were. He was feared, but he was also genuinely liked and loved.

'Do you fancy a bit of work?' he asked.

I did. And Joe didn't have fencing, gardening or tree-felling in mind.

5

ON THE FIRM

That 'bit of work' from Joe, and other jobs that followed not long after, resulted in me soon having a few thousand pounds wrapped around myself. My normal employment got me six quid a week if I was lucky, so it was an enormous amount of money for anyone, let alone a scruff who'd only known poverty. I was advised not to show off and throw it around as it would draw attention to myself, but that was easier said than done. I also kept on my job, as quitting would have been an obvious giveaway that I'd come into money.

Joey Pyle took me to his tailor in London – a man called Barry – who he told me made suits for the Kray twins and other famous people, and helped me get kitted out. I felt like a million dollars in a made-to-measure whistle complete with silk handkerchief and gold cufflinks, all set off by a shiny pair of Loake shoes and a Jermyn Street shirt and tie. I quickly grew to admire Joe, and his mates became my pals – I regarded them as family. For the first time in my life I felt like I belonged, that I was someone. I looked up to Joe. Anything he asked me to do, I would. Without question.

Right from the start, once I was with Joe I was treated very differently. I was on the firm, if you like. I was one of those chaps that people in the boozer looked over at now. Very few people of my age would chance their arm with me, not only because I already had a growing reputation for violence, but they also feared crossing anybody that had any connections to Joey Pyle whatsoever. Gradually, as I got older, more mature and more trusted, Joe introduced me to his wider circle. Practically everyone well known or of any importance I've ever met in my life was through Joe, one way or another.

The promotion of unlicensed fighting was one of the many pies Joe had his fingers in. Years before they became nationally famous outside of unlicensed boxing and criminal circles via their hit books and videos, I met Lenny McLean and Roy Shaw, two of the toughest, roughest men in London. Joe knew them well and had invited them to a function. They were both absolute brutes to look at.

Joe took me to one side. 'Hopefully, it will be OK, Ronnie, but just to let you know, Roy and Lenny hate each other. I mean hate, real hate. Especially Roy. If they start, I'm looking to you to break it up.'

'Are you having a laugh, Joe? Lenny will pull my head off while Roy detaches my fucking legs.'

Joe smiled, put a hand on my shoulder and walked away. I think he was winding me up.

He'd take me up to London to the clubs, a whole new world to me, a million miles from the Red Lion. Dipping in and out of pubs and clubs around Soho, the West End, Mayfair and wider London, we visited the Astor Club, the Bagatelle and the Colony Club, among others. The Colony was said to be Mafia-run, with American actor George Raft once fronting it up. Now I had money I could hold my own, should we have to pay for our drinks. Very often we did not. Everyone knew Joe and rarely was he asked to put his hand in his pocket. He introduced me to characters I'd only heard or read about in the newspapers. It was a dangerous new world, I knew that, but I relished every minute.

It was on one of these trips, to Johnny Saint's club, that I first met Frankie Fraser. Frank was one of the most famous criminals in London and rarely out of prison. It was at the aforementioned Astor Club where Frank and others had a row with Eric Mason, which ended elsewhere with Frank setting about Eric with an axe. His reputation for violence was legendary, and this was before the Richardson trial, where he was alleged to have tied a man up and pulled his teeth out or something similar. It surprised me how small he was.

I was with my mate Cornish, who said to me out the corner of his mouth, 'Is this geezer ever going to buy a drink?'

I must admit Frank did seem a little shy that night about parting company with his cash, but I wasn't expecting Cornish's next line. 'Look, Frank, if you're too small to see over the counter, do you need me to lift you up so you can buy a round?'

Frank didn't smile at first, and I waited for an explosive reaction, but then he laughed, Joe laughed and we all laughed. It was a tense few silent seconds, but Frank went to the bar and got a round in.

Cornish feared nobody. I'd met him in the Red Lion in Sutton. He was a good friend of Joe Pyle's and had recently moved to London from Cornwall. I met Frank many times much later, but we never really hit it off. He wasn't my cup of tea, and I don't think I was his. His son David is a smashing bloke and we get on great.

I bought a 1936 Buick straight-8 car and was very much the man about Cheam. It was incongruous alongside the Morris Minors, Ford Anglias and Triumph Heralds. So much for keeping a low profile. One day I walked into the saloon bar of the Red Lion near the old house and ordered a drink. I had my best pinstripe and tie on, and a very attractive Carol was on my arm. Ginger Bob and my pal Winkle were there with me too. In those days the barmen in some pubs still wore little white waistcoats and provided table service. The youth who served me looked familiar. I studied him a bit more closely.

'Hello, Gerald, or is it David?'

It was one of the twins from school, the snobby gobshites who made me the butt of their jokes and piss-taking.

'It's Gerald, yes. David is serving tables in the other bar.'

He motioned behind him where his twin was lurking, also in his silly white waistcoat. He pretended not to recognise me – or maybe he didn't – and asked who I was.

'It's me, Ronnie. Ronnie Field. From school. Remember?'

Seeing me in a new environment, dressed to the nines, carrying myself with a swagger and confidence, accompanied by a pretty girl on my arm, had confused him. Fish out of water and all that.

'Ronnie. How are you, mate?'

'Yeah, I'm doing great, Gerald. You?'

'Well, yes. Just working here for pin money, you know.'

Gerald seemed embarrassed and a bit wary. I added to his discomfort by pulling the fattest roll of notes he'd ever seen out of my pocket. I peeled off a fiver.

'Get everyone a drink on me,' I said.

'Everyone?' asked Gerald, looking round the pub. There were about twenty-five people in, scattered around.

'Yes, everyone, Gerald.'

Gerald went from table to table obediently taking the orders.

'Oh, Gerald. One for yourself and one for David,' I called out.

It was almost as satisfying as smashing John up with the bat.

Carol and I were married in 1964. I was dressed in my Teddy Boy gear and my brother Ted, fittingly, was my best man. We held the reception at a youth club on the Carshalton Road – now a jujitsu hall – and a good time was had by all. Looking at those wedding pictures, there's one image of me surrounded by my mates, and we're all still Teddy Boys with greased-back hair and velvet collars. It could be 1954 rather than 1964. The Beatles, folk clubs and the new mods, all with their distinctive styles and fashions, were captivating young people across the country, but me and my mates in deepest Cheam and Sutton took no notice. I nearly didn't turn up to the wedding because on my stag night the evening before I drank silly amounts of dark rum and Coke on a pub crawl around Sutton.

We moved into one-room accommodation on the top floor in one of Carol's uncle's houses. He was a successful property developer who owned gaffs all over Sutton and Carshalton. We shared facilities with other tenants and used a gas cooker that was on the landing. As our circumstances improved, we moved down the floors of the house until we settled at the bottom, where we had a separate bedroom, our own kitchen and the garden. The old Victorian house was on Parkhurst Road. It wouldn't be the last place called Parkhurst I'd reside at.

Meanwhile I was mixing legitimate work with criminal forays. There was a character who came in the pub who we nicknamed Collars and Cuffs on account of his flamboyant dress. He was like an Arthur Daley character who had his finger in a lot of pies, and he was a natural deal maker. He was funny and we all liked him. I'd made a new friend by now called Terry Munday, and we were sitting together in the pub chatting one evening when Collars and Cuffs sat down beside us.

'Mind if I join you?'

We didn't. He then asked us if we wanted a job. We did. He explained that a friend of his was a successful and respected local businessman and that his daughter had got wrapped up with a ponce who'd dragged her into his sordid world of drugs and debauchery. He'd led her on to cannabis, pills and ultimately heroin, and had her making what we then quaintly termed 'blue movies'. Pornography. The father was worried that his beautiful beloved daughter was going to end up dead with a needle in her arm. He was desperate. A sorry story indeed.

The businessman was quite clear about what he wanted us to do. We were to rescue his daughter from an address that would be supplied, bash the ponce up, but not too seriously. He wanted to avoid police scrutiny while at the same time frightening the bloke sufficiently that he'd never dare approach his daughter again or seek any sort of revenge or comeback. We were to be paid a grand each, which meant Collars was on for a grand for setting it up, I reckon. Terry and I were well up for it. Low risk, high reward and quite fun in my book.

Terry and I met in his local, the Sailor Prince boozer on Garratt Lane, and drove to the London address we'd been given. We didn't even bother to reccy the gaff, just knocked on the door and barged in when the ponce answered. We told the girl to get her things and went to work on the bloke. He got a good hiding, but I remembered the businessman wanted us to make sure he'd never come back, so I pulled a gun from my belt and warned him. So he didn't think I was bluffing, I whacked him with the butt. I promised him that if I ever saw him again I'd be using the other end of the gun on him. He was shitting himself. As we left the building on a high, I flourished the gun again and shot the windows out of his car. At least, I hope it was his.

The retailer was delighted with our work and several months later invited us to the daughter's wedding, who clearly was making a new, clean, drug-free life for herself. The businessman was still apprehensive about the ponce and thought he might turn up at the function. Terry and I were paid a ton apiece to hang around the entrance and the hall. It was a Jewish wedding, I remember, and the family looked after us well, supplying us with food and drink. Collars turned up, probably to collect his fee, and the businessman came and spoke to us all and thanked us again.

'Can I get you anything?' he said, turning to Collars.

'A ham sandwich would be nice,' said Collars.

'I don't think we have any ham,' said the businessman, smiling politely, 'but I'm sure I can find you something.'

When he left, Terry and I explained to Collars and Cuffs that Jewish people don't eat ham. Didn't he know that? Collars just shrugged.

'That's up to them. I do.'

That day we rescued the girl wasn't the first time I'd handled a gun. I'd been fascinated by them since I was a young kid. I knew the different makes and studied who was firing what in the films. I managed to get hold of some old ones from junk shops and other places, and dismantled them to see how they worked. Returning soldiers from the war bought guns home with them and kids at school would sometimes swap or compare them. I loved the feel of fire-arms, and when I managed to get access to real working pieces I felt empowered. Invincible. I loved a gun.

Me and Terry felt we worked well together, and we decided to hold up a busy shop. We'd personally noted it took a lot of cash. We were getting a taste for the money and the thrill. Terry was a good man and fearless, and I trusted him completely and he me. We watched the gaff for a few days and calculated that the best time to strike would be just before closing. The customers would have thinned out and the maximum amount of cash would be inside the branch. It was no supermarket, but it felt right for our first armed robbery endeavour. We'd enlisted a pal, Winkle, as our geta-way driver, and he sat and waited as Terry and I burst through the door.

I had a sawn-off shotgun in my hand and fired a warning shot into the ceiling, and Terry shouted, 'On the floor. We're not here to hurt you.'

The explosion from my shooter followed by Terry's calm and clear words seemed to do the trick. Terror followed by a comforting statement in quick succession. Three members of staff and perhaps five punters dropped to their knees and then laid on their stomachs, their arms and legs outstretched like starfish. I bent down to collect my cartridge because if one was left, the firearm could be traced. It was an expensive business changing guns.

A future co-blagger of mine had an automatic shotgun, and as he fired he'd stretch out his arm, open his hand, catch the cartridge and stuff it in his pocket in one swift movement. I didn't even know he was there when he first did it, and the discharge of his gun made me jump. 'Fucking hell …' and I nearly said his name. He said sorry, but he was worried I was taking so long. I explained there was a lot of money to be picked up. Normally, he sat in the car.

Back to the shop.

'Open the safe,' commanded Terry, as I trained the gun around the room like they did in the films.

A member of staff obliged, and Terry knelt and threw the contents of the safe into the kit bag we'd brought with us. We then walked backwards out of the door, walked fast around the corner to the car that Winkle had fired up and we were away. The whole thing had taken about four minutes, and when we counted up the cash it amounted to a couple of thousand pounds. It was a good enough haul, the blag was executed well, nobody got hurt and nobody got nicked. Terry and I decided that armed robbery was the game for us. Besides, everybody was at it.

Armed robbery is old as the hills. A caveman bashing another over the head with his club and relieving him of his freshly hunted bison from over his shoulders is arguably the earliest example. Later there was Robin Hood, who robbed the rich and gave to the poor, allegedly. I bet he kept plenty for himself. I could argue that we were robbing from the rich (banks) and giving to the poor (me), but I won't.

Then in the seventeenth and eighteenth centuries there was the phenomenon of highwaymen, who were the first armed robbers to take up firearms. There are plenty of parallels with the highwaymen and my era: the carriages, caravans and stagecoaches they ordered to 'stand and deliver' were the Securicor and Group 4 vans, the little eye mask was the balaclava and stocking, and the blunderbuss was the sawn-off.

Dick Turpin was the most celebrated highwayman, and unlike Robin Hood he definitely did exist. Dick was famous for riding from London to York on his horse Black Bess, and it was in York where he was detained, imprisoned and hanged. French-born Claude Du Vall was another highwayman who captured the imagination of the public and poets alike a few years before Dick. Du Vall was known for his sharp dressing, impeccable manners and Gallic charm. Legend has it that during one robbery he insisted on dancing with a female victim after relieving her husband of all his valuables. His charisma, though, was not enough to dodge the noose, and he was hanged at Tyburn Tree in London in 1670.

In the nineteenth century the epicentre of armed robbery shifted to America, where my childhood heroes Jessie and Frank James achieved legendary status robbing banks and holding up trains. Jessie's life as a fugitive ended prematurely when he was shot in the back by the coward Robert Ford. His brother Frank, however, was one of the few celebrity outlaws to make old age. He died aged seventy-two after some years living a quiet life as a shoe salesman.

The first half of the twentieth century saw the arrival of a new breed of robbers in America, many spawned by the desperate economic situation of the Great Depression in the 1920s and 1930s. Despite – or because of – their use of automatic weapons and the rising level of fatalities in their raids, many have been mythologised and glamorised by Hollywood: the Barker family, Baby Face Nelson and his occasional partner in crime John Dillinger, Bonnie and Clyde, and Butch Cassidy. Butch and his 'Wild Bunch' gang robbed the San Miguel Valley Bank in 1889 of $21,000, the equivalent of over $600,000 in today's money. You couldn't have met two nicer guys, who liked nothing more than riding around on bicycles with pretty girls on their crossbars than Butch and his sidekick the Sundance Kid, if Paul Newman and Robert Redford's screen portrayals are to be believed. Ma Barker, the matriarch of the Barker clan, was immortalised in a song by 1970s pop band Boney M. Lucky for them she wasn't around to take them to task for misspelling her name and calling her Ma Baker.

John Dillinger went out with a bang – excuse the pun. His crime spree lasted some years, and J. Edgar Hoover, the head of the FBI, made it his personal business to hunt him down and take him out – dead or alive. He was deemed Public Enemy Number One. The federal agents finally cornered Dillinger as he left the Biograph Theatre after watching a Clark Gable crime film called *Manhattan Melodrama* in 1934. They gunned him down, and such was his celebrity that after his body was moved bystanders dipped their handkerchiefs in his blood for keepsakes. These days they'd be flogging them on eBay before the blood was dry.

Back home, the armed robbery industry really took off in the 1960s, with the Great Train Robbery of 1963 inspiring a generation of thieves. In true Jesse James style, a bunch of London villains managed to stop a train in rural Buckinghamshire at night and relieve it of £2.6m, an incredible *£50m* at today's values. Even after it was divvied out between at least twelve of the robbers, that's around £3m each.

The whole operation was planned and directed in a masterly way by Bruce Reynolds, and nobody was killed in its execution. It made the government look stupid, not only for allowing a train carrying such sums to travel around the country unprotected but because the state had been outwitted by a group of uneducated crooks. Not an Eton old boy among them. The media and the government were outraged and furious, but the truth is most of the general public privately admired the caper. In the British annals of crime, the fascination with the Great Train Robbers has only been surpassed by the legend of the Kray twins and the story of Jack the Ripper. Unfortunately for the robbers, they were the subject of the biggest police operation ever mounted up to that point and none really got to enjoy the spoils of their daring for any length of time. At least, the ones we know about didn't.

The train robbery was at the upper end of the armed robbery industry. Most armed robberies were being carried out on suburban bank branches, post offices and betting shops, along with industrial premises, where wages were being snatched with increasing regularity. In 1968 there were twelve bank robberies in inner London, for example; by 1972 that had risen to sixty-five. That equated to more than one every six days in the central London area alone. Taking all the reconnaissance trips into consideration, there were possibly more armed robbers knocking about London's high streets than there were traffic wardens at various times. In 1969 it was estimated that banks lost £3m to armed snatches. That's £140m in today's money. If we'd all put our hauls together back in 1969, we'd have had enough dosh to have bought the entire Manchester United and Manchester City football teams.

With Terry we were soon robbing betting shops, banks and post offices regularly. I had a sawn-off pump-action shotgun and an automatic among my weaponry. My favourite was the pump-action sawn-off. When you pumped the gun again after having shot the ceiling of the bank in, for example, the clicking noise and the sinister movement electrified the branch as the cowering people in an already terrified room were reminded of the threat. It certainly deterred many have-a-go heroes.

I was good at actually sawing off the shotguns. If you cut them too short the spring wouldn't work. I learned that the hard way when I let off into a door at a bank; the spring had gone, the gun wouldn't reload and I had no more shots. I'd sawn the butt off too much. Luckily for me, I was the only person present besides Terry who could be sure of that. He wasn't happy with me that day. It was a serious mistake that could have got us both seven years.

I always remember the first bank. It was a step up from a betting shop and there was more money for a start. We picked a Friday, because in those days everyone got paid in cash at the end of the week, so we figured Securicor would be bringing more cash than usual – and we were right. We simply waited for the guards to deliver and leave the branch, then we burst in through the doors, I leapt over the counter – which in those days was half protected behind reinforced glass, just some higher glass to get over – and tossed the bags over to Terry. It was so easy. We got one of our biggest hauls that morning.

There was normally three of us on a raid. A driver, me and a partner. Sometimes two would suffice – the driver and me – but that was cutting corners, and you opened yourself up to more risk. You can't be everywhere at once. Occasionally if the counter area was more secure, I had to put a gun to the head of a customer and tell the bank teller to come round and open the door. Later the third man was required, as often I'd have to go down to the vault or another part of the bank to get the money, and so my partner needed to be upstairs to subdue the staff and any customers. I found out later that two of my sisters, Pat and Dalla, had worked in banks, and Pat had worked her way up to be manager. She'd spent time at a Cheam branch. Thank fuck I never robbed it. That would have been problematical.

The security industry boomed in the 1960s and 70s. Blue vans marked Securicor, Security Express, Group 4 and other names were as familiar sights on our road network as the supermarket food delivery vans today. They parked up on our high streets as they delivered, and collected cash to and from our banks in those heady days before electronic transfer. Guards in their uniforms with visor helmets were a more familiar sight than a policeman on the beat. It became a thing to hold up the guards as they walked in and out of the bank branches clutching money bags. The guards were unarmed, and the threat of a sawn-off shotgun being waved at them would normally be enough to persuade them to part company with the cash. After all it was only a job, and it wasn't their money. However, there was always the occasional nutter who wouldn't let go of the bags. They didn't know who was on the other end of the shooter. Some robbers drew the line at shooting a guard, some didn't.

We'd follow the vans on their rounds and work out their routes, note the times and days they came and went. At first it was easy, often like taking candy from a baby. The guards would hand bags of cash over the counter to the staff and the bags would sit there for a moment. As soon as the guards were out of sight we'd storm in, and I'd generally aim at the ceiling and fire. Going round or over the counter and taking the bags was normally easy. Of course, we preferred the first drop bank as there was more money at the beginning of the day than any time later on.

Soon we got to thinking about the money inside the van. If you waited for the final collection there'd be the cash from several branches in one place. The reward-to-risk ratio was increased several times. One hold-up, several hauls. The driver would seal himself in his cab, two guards would approach the bank together and inside the van was a safe full of cash just waiting for us. However, they made the safes stronger and stronger, and the men did not have the codes. It became harder and harder to blow them open.

Leafing through the evening paper one day I spotted a job advertisement for a security guard for the leading company at the time, Securicor. I decided to apply. To my surprise I was quickly invited for interview. I put on my best suit and took the train up to London with all the commuters. In those days some of them really did wear bowler hats. I bought a copy of *The Times* so my interviewers thought I was abreast of current affairs and educated. I went into the company's plush headquarters and sat down in front of an interview committee. I sailed through it.

'Why do you want to become a security guard, Mr Field?'

'I'm going nowhere building fences and tree lopping, sir. Just want to develop my career.'

'Are you aware of the risks?'

Only too well, I could have replied.

'Yes, sir. There are risks in felling trees too,' I shrugged.

The panel smiled.

'We'll let you know, Mr Field. Thank you for attending today.'

I knew they liked me. I assume they checked out my criminal record. Remarkably, I still didn't have one yet. A few days later a letter arrived offering me the job. Soon I did an induction course and was then fitted out for a neat Securicor uniform, complete with cap and helmet. I was in gainful employment – it was enough to make a man go straight. I did a couple of weeks in the control room and then they told me I was to go out on the road. I felt like a secret agent. Field's the name. Ronald Field.

Travelling around London in the van, I familiarised myself with routes and practices. I got a thrill entering the occasional branch I'd been in before with a stocking over my head, and wondered what I'd do if a blagger jumped out in front of me and told me to hand over the bag. I was careful not to say anything like 'Get on the floor' or 'Hand the cash over' or 'Don't panic, love, we just want the money', just in case some vigilant bank teller recognised my voice. Back in the van, the in-vehicle safes fascinated me. Heavy and fortified as they were, their backs were the side panel of the vehicle. It occurred to me that a car sunroof fitter could cut through that with the ease of a knife through butter. It was a serious security flaw.

I spoke to a few colleagues about my observations, but before I could put my ideas into practice I got called up for jury service at Kingston Crown Court. It was a strange case where some men had thrown some missiles at an umpire at the Oval. I couldn't understand why it was being heard in the Crown Court – the defendants were clearly guilty, and the jury was almost unanimous. There was only one dissenter. Me. I did try to emulate Henry Fonda in *Twelve Angry Men* and talk my fellow jurors round, but to no avail. Sorry, chaps.

Either my observations about the in-van safes had been passed around or others were thinking along the same lines, but by the time I finished my jury service some of the more sophisticated gangs were already opening security vans and putting a hole in the safes like opening a tin of beans. They were doing this in record time with cutting equipment.

The banks and the security companies were forever coming up with new ideas and technologies to thwart us, and we blaggers were forever thinking of ways to get around them. Those were the days – such fun. We were beginning to think we were the 'A' Team as we weren't getting caught, not even close. We spent money freely and lived charmed lives, but we didn't brag or try to take on too much. I started to look upon it as a real job and took pride in 'going to work'. I thought it would last for ever.

6

OUTLAWS

I wasn't out blagging all the time; I was taking on other work too. Some via Joe, some I was picking up elsewhere. One example was when Joe was approached by a publican in Redhill who'd just taken over new premises. He was a law-abiding small businessman just trying to make a living and was being leant on by a couple of local criminals demanding protection money or else. Joe said to the man who didn't know who to turn to, do you want us to sort it?

The situation was explained, and me, Cornish and another pal went down to deepest Surrey on the day we were told these characters were turning up with palms outstretched. We were in our best clobber and looked the part. We got there first and waited patiently. Eventually two men in their thirties wearing T-shirts and jeans swaggered in and took up position at the bar. The staff made themselves busy elsewhere. Cornish and I took them firmly by the arms, said, 'Could you come with us, please,' and led them to a kitchen area through a door out of sight of the bar. They allowed us to lead them – I guess they thought we were Old Bill. Once the door was shut, I produced an automatic pistol, flipped out a bullet, and held it between finger and thumb in front of one man's face.

'Swallow it,' I demanded.

The man was immediately terrified.

'What?'

'Swallow it,' I repeated.

The fact that Cornish had the other man's hand clasped in his on a chopping board and was asking me if he should cut his fingers off helped persuade him. He took the bullet from me and swallowed it in one quivering gulp.

'Now, if you ever come here again demanding money the next one's coming straight out the barrel and blasting through your chest.'

I poked his chest bone.

'Got it?'

The man was on the verge of tears.

'Got it,' he said.

Joe had stressed to me right from the beginning, 'In this game, Ron, you have to be worse than the other mush,' and he was right.

Taking money from publicans – or people trying to, like this pair of clowns – was a much more widespread practice than people realised. In Greater London, at least, I reckon more pubs than not had some arrangement or other, whether it be a brown envelope once a month or – more subtly – free drinks and hospitality to firm members when they turned up. Joe told me that he checked in with the Redhill landlord later and the two would-be gangsters hadn't been in since. They'd probably not been out of their gaffs since, I reckon. Joe asked the landlord how much they were asking.

'They wanted £100 a week, Joe!'

'Well, you just saved yourself £50 a week,' Joe replied.

We also did a bit of debt management, me and Cornish. If somebody owed some money, we'd go and collect. Normally people paid up, or at least agreed to a payment plan. If they wouldn't settle, then we might smash their legs up depending on how genuine they were. If we weren't firm, people would start thinking we had nothing in the tank and we wouldn't be very effective. There are people out there who will refuse to pay a bill, or take on a debt with no intention of ever honouring it. The person who's owed the money often has nowhere to turn and are sometimes threatened for having the temerity to ask for their money back. That's when they might turn to us. The building trade were one of our regular customers. Their clients refused to pay for work done, calling out snagging errors as an excuse. It was – and I guess still is – common.

It was rare for people not to pay. In fact, once certain names were mentioned as being involved in the collection of a debt, the money owed was usually forthcoming. I'd do what I could to avoid violence, but there were the occasional times when a debt dodger didn't take you seriously and I had to up the game. A couple of times I sneaked into a man's house and left a used cartridge on his pillow as he slept. This normally did the trick.

Life with Cornish was never dull. When the flower lady came into the pub proffering a single rose for an extortionate quid, he'd buy the lot off her in one go and present them with a flourish to the nearest pretty lady. Like me, he spent money as quickly as he stole it. But he could turn on a sixpence. Woe betide those stupid enough to cross him.

Early on I witnessed the power of being 'on the firm' when I was pulled over in my car and breathalysed. The bag went blue, or whatever colour indicated you'd drunk over the limit, and a young copper not much older than me smirked as he told me I was nicked for drunken driving. But when he started to manhandle me, I walloped him on the jaw, grabbed him around the neck and spread him over the bonnet of my car as I throttled him. We grappled for a bit, with the policeman's arms thrashing, then an ambulance pulled up and two ambulancemen jumped out in their blue shirts and peaked caps. They weren't called paramedics then. Talk about solidarity among the emergency services; one of them clumped me over the head with a gas bottle and I was subdued.

At the station I was told I was going to be charged with the attempted murder of a police officer. This was a serious charge, which would normally bring a big lump of porridge. The situation was fast escalating out of my control. I hadn't attempted to murder a policeman – I'd wrestled with one. Words were had in higher places, though, and I was eventually charged with the lesser count of assault. I was assured that a thousand pounds had changed hands. At court I received two months' imprisonment, suspended for one year. There was no mention of the drink-driving. It was a stupid, reckless thing to do, and Joe wasn't best pleased.

Life by the mid- to late-60s was going swimmingly. London was swinging. Fashion was all-important. Suavely dressed mods and leather-jacketed rockers paraded in huge numbers on holiday beaches, teenagers walked around clasping transistor radios to their ears from which the sounds of the Beatles, the Small Faces and the Kinks wafted out, and Steve McQueen, Clint Eastwood, Sean Connery, Sophia Loren and Jane Fonda were drawing the punters into the cinemas. The England football team were responsible for the biggest surge in national pride since we beat the Germans in 1945 by beating them in 1966 in the World Cup final at Wembley. David Bailey was bouncing around, capturing it all on camera. Some of his most famous photographs were of the notorious Kray twins, who became icons of the decade as much as any other cultural figure. The fifteen minutes of fame Andy Warhol promised everyone has lasted fifty-five years for the twins, and we're still counting. The 60s was all about rebellion after all, and they didn't come much more rebellious that Ron and Reg Kray.

Joey Pyle talked about them a lot and he knew them both well. I thought I might meet them on our trips to London, but they didn't seem to inhabit Soho, the West End and the clubs we went to at that time. They were busy with their own clubs and preferred the familiarity of their own manor, the East End of London.

They had, though, pulled off a cheeky hustle in nearby Epsom, my birthplace, that was often talked about. In 1958 Ronnie was criminally detained at Long Grove mental hospital for a period. Long Grove was one of a cluster of six such hospitals that were dotted around the rural outskirts of Epsom town. The surroundings were bucolic and seemed a million miles – not fifteen – from the bustling, sometimes dangerous pubs and clubs of Whitechapel, Bethnal Green and Mile End.

Reggie was concerned that Ronnie was being pharmaceutically neutered and worried that his brother might never get out of what in those days we unkindly called the 'loony bin' or 'nuthouse'. One Sunday Reg went to visit Ron, and wore a suit and a raincoat. Ron had been told to wear a suit too. They sat together, sipped tea and chatted. When Ron stepped into the corridor to get a refill of tea he took Reggie's coat. He simply put the mac on and walked out of the hospital into a waiting car. The male nurses assumed it was Reggie finishing his visit and now leaving. When fifteen minutes later Reggie innocently asked the nurse if he'd seen his brother because he'd gone to make a cup of tea and not returned, the staff knew they'd been had and phoned the police.

After that the Krays appeared in the newspapers regularly, often photographed with celebrities at charity events. I read about them, and heard more on the criminal grapevine. In

1966 they went on television to be interviewed; they were going mainstream. Most people in the know knew it was Ronnie that had shot and killed south London face George Cornell in the Blind Beggar pub in Whitechapel, and that the twins had sprung Frank Mitchell, the so-called 'Mad Axeman', from Dartmoor Prison and then got shot of him. 'The Sun Ain't Gonna Shine Anymore' by the Walker Brothers was apparently playing on the jukebox when Ronnie unloaded on George. Strange that people in the pub could remember that but couldn't recall a murder. The papers had a field day while Frank Mitchell was on the loose, terrifying their readers with the image of a hulking giant skulking in shop doorways caressing his sharp axe.

The following year Reg killed a local villain known as Jack 'the Hat' McVitie. Jack has been portrayed in Kray folklore as an out-of-control, drugged-up petty crook, but Joe always told me he was an all-right bloke and nobody's fool. I remember Joe telling me that Jack had lived in Sutton for a while. The Krays' activities were well known, and it was seen as an affront to the police and the authorities that they were able to operate and kill in plain sight. Scotland Yard unleashed their smallest but most tenacious detective, Leonard 'Nipper' Read, onto the case. He was possibly one of the few senior Scotland Yard detectives at the time not tainted by the stench of police corruption. In 1968 he arrested the twins and others in the 'firm' for the murders of Jack McVitie, George Cornell and Frank Mitchell. The following year the twins were sentenced at the Old Bailey to thirty years apiece. There had never been a trial like it. The security and fanfare as the defendants were taken to and from court was like they presented a threat to the nation greater than the Soviet Union.

I asked Joe once when I was still very young and learning the game, 'How come the Krays are so famous and get all the publicity, and nobody writes about our firm?'

Joe tapped the side of nose and winked. 'Let them have as much of the limelight as they want. We're happy in the shadows with the money, eh Ronnie?'

The twins' older brother Charlie was collateral damage in all this. The Old Bill were determined that the whole 'empire', as they called it, be brought down, and he was charged with being an accessory to the murder of Jack the Hat and with involvement in the disposal of Jack's body. He copped ten years, essentially for being a brother of the twins. Charlie might have been a wide boy, as they used to say, but he was not an integral part of the twins' criminal enterprises, and although having had a decent career as a boxer he wasn't a man readily disposed to violence. If he was, plenty would have gone into print and to the documentary makers with stories by now. He strived to succeed in legitimate business, but his surname continually dragged him back to the criminal margins.

In 1975 George Davis became the most famous armed robber on the planet for a short while. He'd received a harsh twenty-year sentence for a wages snatch at the London Electricity Board offices in Ilford, east London. A guard had been shot and injured, but the authorities' frustration at not being able to keep a lid on these incessant armed robberies was probably reflected in the length of the sentence. Not many got that amount of bird for murder.

The problem was, George wasn't on this particular job. The police wouldn't have cared about that – as far as they were concerned he was an active armed robber, and if he got banged up for a job he didn't do after getting away with dozens he did do, that was a technicality. That's how the Old Bill looked at things in those days. To an extent some criminals thought the same way. In prison there really are plenty of inmates who are away for crimes they didn't actually commit, but because there's so much they've got away with that they don't want revisiting, they don't lose too much sleep over it and get on with the bird. I'm reminded of the Morecambe and Wise sketch where Eric grabs conductor André Previn by the lapels and says, 'I'm playing all the right notes, but not necessarily in the right order, sunshine.' In prison, they're detaining mainly the right criminals, but not necessarily for the right crimes.

So, even though they knew what George did to supplement his minicab-driving living, his friends and families weren't having it. This was a twenty-year sentence, not a three-year term where he'd only serve two with good behaviour – and these were the best years of his life. His plucky wife Rose and determined best friend Peter Chappell launched the 'George Davis Is Innocent OK' campaign, where they daubed the slogan all over London in defiant white paint. Some of the graffiti still survives today. Most famously, though, the protestors dug up the cricket pitch at Headingley, meaning the Test match between England and Australia had to be abandoned, denying England a chance to regain the Ashes. The incident pushed the IRA and the Bay City Rollers off the front pages, and Chappell served time for this one.

The police evidence against George was demonstrably flawed and, two years into his sentence, the Home Secretary Roy Jenkins released him, although he stopped short of pardoning or exonerating him. George had to wait to 2011 for a court to officially overturn his conviction for the LEB job. However, in 1978 he pleaded guilty to an armed robbery the previous year at the Bank of Cyprus on the Seven Sisters Road. He'd not been out long and was driving the getaway vehicle. A gun was discharged and a guard was clubbed. George got a fifteen-year stretch, reduced on appeal to eleven. This time there was no campaign to free him. The moral high ground had crumbled beneath him. I'm surprised that no graffiti artists with a sense of humour and cockney savvy ever went around town crossing the 'Innocent' out in the daubings and replacing it with 'Guilty'.

I had no qualms about the work I was doing. I knew it was legally and morally wrong, but I'd never really been exposed to much in life that had made me consider morality too often. I was an angry, violent and dangerous young man, and I didn't give a fuck. It wasn't morally wrong in our circles, by the way. Robbing banks was not taking *people's* money in our eyes. No current account holder suffered financially as a result of our activities. The banks didn't even lose out. What we stole would have ultimately been covered by the insurance industry. We didn't really think about it. Banks and insurance companies were just two cheeks of the same arse, agents of the Establishment that had done fuck-all for the likes of us, an Establishment that greedily kept the wealth and the land of the country to itself, passing it down the generations so us peasants could not get our grubby mitts on it. Us plebs were good for digging the coal, building the roads, fighting the wars, but we were still looked down on from a great height. Fuck that for a game of soldiers. You swallow it, I don't. That's how I looked at it then.

Another thing was that our active enemy in this dangerous game of cat and mouse were the police. Well, we knew then what the average man and woman would only know later, and that was that the police were bent. Corrupt. Bad. The public had this image of gentle, friendly, honest coppers like Sergeant George Dixon in TV's *Dixon of Dock Green* or Bert Lynch in *Z Cars*. And it was not just a few bad apples, as they like to claim. There were orchards full of the fuckers.

Scotland Yard, at least, was a hotbed of bent coppers and corruption. It all came out in the 1970s, but we knew this for years, and I reckon it always was so. I'm not just talking about fitting people up, and encouraging and using grasses, but demanding and taking money from people like us, even setting up jobs from which they'd take a cut.

The head of the Flying Squad, the division tasked with dealing with armed robbery during my most active periods, was an officer called Detective Chief Superintendent Kenneth Drury. He was double corrupt and even went on holiday with the Soho villain and pornographer Jimmy Humphreys. Paid by Jimmy, of course. Drury was finally convicted in 1977 and got eight years. A whole raft of his minions also went down with him, as well as officers from the Obscene Publications Squad, who were raking off hundreds of thousands from the Soho sex shops. If the top men in an organisation are bent, that will infect the culture and filter down.

I was with Joe one day in Johnny Saint's club, and a man came in alone and sat with us. I knew he was a cozzer – you could normally tell – and I sussed by Joe's body language too. He bristled and stiffened up as the man sat next to him. He hated most Old Bill.

After some forced pleasantries, the copper said, 'You know what, Joe? You're the only one who doesn't pay us. You know the rules, Joe.'

'You know what?' and Joe said his name, so they'd obviously crossed paths before. 'Bullets cost money.'

The defective detective shook his head, pushed away his unfinished drink and walked out.

'Tosser,' said Joe to me.

Years later I saw the man's face on television and on the front of books. Many corruption allegations were laid at his door, but to my knowledge this particular one was never brought down.

So, in our opened eyes the police were as bad if not worse than us, and we never laboured under the illusion that they were the good guys, like everyone else did. Fitting up people was a well-known practice. I knew more than one mate who'd been stopped by police and had an 'armed robber kit' chucked into his car. This was a bag with a ski mask, a cosh, a gun and some bullets all handily inside. Joe Public would never believe that police planted 'evidence', but they did, and they did it brazenly.

On top of all of this justification, whether valid or not, I was determined never to be poor again. I loved the sharp suits, the camaraderie with the chaps, the thrills and spills and the good life. I loved nice things. They made me feel worthy. I'd made something of myself. The only way I was going to give that up was if it was taken away from me forcibly.

7

SUMMER OF '76

I was happily married. In 1967 we had a daughter who tragically died. When the vicar in the hospital made the mistake of telling me it was God's will and he had 'chosen' her, I set about him. You don't need all that religious bollocks at a time like that. I didn't, anyway. In 1968 our Sadie was born. She was – and is – the apple of my eye. I bought a house in Sutton to house my new family. I walked into the estate agents' office after having seen some pleasing pictures in the shop window. I'd been grafting legitimately that afternoon – chopping trees, I believe – and the estate agent didn't like the cut of my jib. He barely looked up as I stood in front of his desk, my scruffiness and relative youth having made his mind up that I was going to offer to clean the windows or something.

'I'd like to buy that house, please,' I said, politely, pointing at the picture.

The besuited agent, who was probably not that much older than me, looked at me with mild curiosity.

'It's on the market for £7,000. You'd need a mortgage in place.'

What he stopped himself adding was, 'Now, piss off and let me get on with my work.'

'I don't need a mortgage, mate. I'll pay cash.'

His attitude was annoying me.

'Want a deposit?' I added, pulling half the total price of the house from my pocket in rolls bound up by big sturdy brown elastic bands.

'Please sit down, sir. Would you like a cup of tea?'

It's sir, now. Money really does talk – the estate agent was my best pal all of a sudden. He guided me through the buying process, and we were in our new home within a few weeks. The day after getting the keys, having paid for the house by robbing banks, I went out and robbed a post office to furnish the gaff.

I was on the pavement – as we called it back then – almost weekly, and sometimes our little firm would even do a job in the morning and another in the afternoon. We didn't put a foot wrong and considered ourselves the business at what we did. The thrill and excitement of pulling a lady's brown stocking over my face or donning a ski mask was unmatched. I knew we were going to work. The ski mask wasn't essential, but it frightened the granny out of people and encouraged compliance. I even winced when I looked in the mirror. The supergrass Derek 'Bertie' Smalls, who was nevertheless a very good armed robber, is quoted as saying:

The nervous tension I used to feel before a job didn't stay with me all the time. Once I start I feel completely calm, one hundred per cent, everything becomes brilliant to me ... it's like the sun coming out from behind a cloud.

I never felt that nervous tension Bertie the grass refers to, just excitement and a keenness to get going, but that feeling of calm once inside a bank I can identify with.

I met Bertie once, maybe twice, in a club or a pub. He seemed a nice enough fella to me, and I was shocked when he went supergrass. But he was planning it all along. It was his Get Out of Jail Free card. I say that, because he wrote everything down – which you don't do unless you're planning to use that information at some time in the future. I consider myself lucky I never went to work with him.

Bertie certainly had bottle. I read that he took his wife and child down the south coast one day. Dumped them near the beach and said he had some business to attend to, then went off and joined up with his firm and robbed a bank in the seaside town, just as planned. Job done, he went back to the beach and building sandcastles with his wife and kid. That was cheeky. Holidaymakers must have wondered who the fat bloke in the deckchair with a stocking over his face was. Obviously there was a price on Bertie's head after he did his dirty deal with the police and put dozens of his colleagues and pals in the nick, but remarkably nobody ever caught up with him. This is strange, as I heard more than once he was living in Croydon. I'm told he died a few years back. But did he? I wouldn't put anything past Bertie Smalls.

A few of the lads that were on remand courtesy of Bertie staged an audacious breakout from Brixton Prison. Mickey 'the Fish' Sammon, Bruce Brown, Danny Allpress and Jimmy Wilkinson were among the fifteen inmates who hijacked a skip truck that had entered the prison. One of them brandished a pretend revolver fashioned from a bar of soap and coated with black shoe polish. They nearly made it, as they smashed the gates open with the truck, but the machinery on the back got tangled up. They had no choice but to leg it but unfortunately were all recaptured.

There were four of us on our firm now: me, Terry, Pat and Colin. Pat would go out and nick the car the day before – or even later, on the morning of the job – and he'd sometimes take two: one for the immediate getaway and one for plotting up for the changeover car we'd jump into to throw people off the trail. Occasionally we used three cars in total. Pat had a slide hammer that he'd use to take the ignition out, and then he did something clever with the wires. It was a mystery to me. I had trouble operating the pull-out choke. Then we'd either walk in different directions to our safe house for divvying up the cash or get in our own motors. We often used the upstairs rooms of a friendly publican.

Normally only Terry and I would be armed. Pat needed both hands as he was the scooper or the 'bag man'. Bending down, scooping up the bags or bundles of banded notes and throwing them in our holdall or cricket bag was an important role. He was also adept with the bolt cutters, cutting the chain on the security guard's wrist. Now and then, not wanting to be shot, the guard would enthusiastically help. I'd normally get up high, jumping on the counter or something. This way I could see everyone, and everyone could see me and more importantly my shooter. This was after I'd blown the obligatory hole in the ceiling, wall or door. It was important to control the situation. Terry would likewise be hovering around the front-door area should anybody try to make a bolt for it or come stumbling in.

Colin refused point blank to carry a gun. He didn't agree with it. He wasn't really cut out to be an armed robber, but he was a bloody good getaway driver and we valued him on the team. The guns would be returned to their hiding place, which was nowhere near any of us. We stashed them on a farm some miles away. Counting the money as we took it out in the room over a pub and then sharing it out while drinking a bottle of vodka was a great high. At the end we'd leave separately – our spoils in a bag or secreted about our person – and head home. A good day's work.

My dear mum died of cancer in 1968 in the West Middlesex Hospital. The poor woman didn't even make sixty years of age, and most of those years were unhappy and miserable. I was and am desperately sad about her life – she got a raw deal. Me, Pat, Cissy and my brother-in-law Tony were at her bedside when she went, and I'm grateful for that. Her funeral wasn't well attended. Why would it be? She didn't have much of a social life and her illness kept her indoors for years.

As we approached the cemetery, I remember as we passed him in the funeral car, a man – a complete stranger – stopped walking, stood erect, removed his cap and bowed his head. This random mark of respect for my mother really touched me. I'll never forget that. Respect and empathy to others like that was common then. It's all gone now. Cars overtake and weave in and out of the family funeral cortege, breaking it up. I feel like leaping out the funeral car, dragging the drivers out their seat and battering them. But you have to behave yourself at a funeral, don't you?

The old man followed Mum in 1971. He made sixty-three years of age, not considered as premature then as it would be now. Cancer got him too. I was with him at the West Brompton Hospital when he went. Just me and Tony. Dad and I were getting along at the time of his death, but I always had some mixed feelings when I thought about the life he gave his wife. And us, I suppose. Looking back now, my old man was an arsehole, I must admit. If we ever get around to giving him a gravestone, I might get some sticks of gelignite carved on the stone.

By the mid-1970s things were still holding up. Carol and I had our own house, a new Jaguar or Rover V8 3.5-litre coupe every year and more cash than a man could dream of. I loved the Rovers because CID used them too. For a while I even had a Harrods bank account. I don't believe they had many branches, but if they had I'd have still robbed them. I'd have got a perverse thrill out of robbing back money I'd just paid in.

I'd been a serious criminal for almost fifteen years and never been banged up or properly nicked even. We were one of the best blagging teams in town, I don't care what anyone says. It was all too easy. Because we were getting away with it, nobody knew us. That's the irony about crime – the most successful villains are anonymous. You only hear about the ones that fail.

But Carol was unhappy. She didn't approve of what I did, even though she never asked about it or mentioned it, and I never discussed my other life with her. But she knew, she must have. She witnessed some very violent and shocking things in pubs and clubs, and was freaked out when I sometimes came home covered in blood – normally not mine. She didn't like some of the villains and faces I was knocking around with. Like me, she loved Joe, but some of the others gave her the shivers. Eventually it all became too much for her and we parted. We did get back together for a while, but the relationship was essentially over. She kept the house, I kept the stocking and the sawn-off.

I was relaxed about my chosen profession. In fact, I was proud. In the criminal hierarchy, armed robbers were much respected. It was a game where the stakes were high, and the majority of criminals didn't have the stomach for it. Few had the bottle required, especially when the police took to interrupting the robberies on the pavement and ambushing us. They were armed too now and weren't shy of shooting first.

Although we used guns, most of us armed robbers weren't going to plug you for looking at us the wrong way, like some violent criminals. If comparisons were to be made with sport, we were the Formula One drivers. That's how we were regarded among our own. I loved being on the pavement, and I never mugged a man or woman on the street, nor did I ever break into a person's house to rob them or beat up an innocent person. I detested that sort of criminal. They gave us a bad name, and nothing upset us more than being lumped in with the scum.

Working with and for Joey Pyle was also something I valued very highly. The older I got, the more I realised what a special person he was. He spoke words of wisdom, was a diplomat and a smart businessman. Had he been born in different circumstances – in a different area at a different time – he'd have been the managing director of a company quoted on the Stock Exchange, I'm sure. I had complete faith in Joe. He never told me to do anything – he asked. And I never turned him down. Except on one occasion. Later in life Joe got himself a little dog. It was a poodle, I think. Harley, he called it. Looked ridiculous. I don't know what on earth came over him. One day at his house he handed me a dainty little lead.

'I've got some calls to make, Ronnie. Could you give the dog a walk over the park, please?'

I had my best suit on. We were local and most people knew me. I just couldn't do it.

'I'm sorry, Joe. But no. I'm not walking around the streets with that pathetic little thing mincing along behind me.'

'That's my dog you're talking about,' said Joe, only half joking.

People talk about the Krays, the Richardsons and the gangsters that went before and came after, but Joe was just as active, just as effective, just as firm, but managed to keep his head just under the parapet. The proof was in the pudding; he'd stayed out of prison since the Cooney case and had avoided serious conflict with other firms. To me he was like the Marlon Brando Don Corleone character from *The Godfather* – wise, firm and fair. In middle age he even began to look like an Italian don. He mainly kept out of the media, and the press only sniffed him out when they ran out of other faces to splash over their front pages after all the Krays, Richardsons and Frasers of this world had been locked up.

I met another girl, Jackie, whose father was Johnny the Egg Man, a Del Boy type on Surrey Street market in Croydon, and we were together for a time, marrying in 1976. We first met in the Red Lion in Sutton. Where else? Johnny the Egg Man turned me over, actually. I wore a lot of jewellery in those days. Put Bobby George to shame. Chunky identity bracelets, rope chains around the neck, rings on most fingers and Rolex watches. I studiously avoided magnets.

Well, Johnny the Egg Man particularly liked a solitaire ring I owned and asked if he could borrow it to wear to some function he'd been invited to. He wanted to make an impression, he claimed. I should have known better, because when I asked for it back Johnny swore blind he'd lost it. I didn't believe him for one minute, but couldn't prove anything. I was convinced he'd flogged it, but he was Jackie's old man, so I didn't turn up the heat. Later, Jackie was innocently showing me some Christmas wedding photographs at her parents' house while I'd been away. My eyes alighted on her father and his hand resting on the arm of his chair. There was my solitaire ring. Bold as brass. I didn't say anything to Jackie, but I certainly made an impression on Johnny the Egg Man when I saw him later.

However, my days of living the high life were about to end abruptly. My long criminal purple patch of excitement, fast cars, pubs and clubs was going to be rudely interrupted in the long, hot summer of 1976. It was June. If it wasn't, it felt like June. We'd never had weather like it. The sun came up early each morning and didn't go to bed until ten o'clock at night. Tarmac roads melted, people fried eggs on car bonnets because they could, and the only water that wasn't in short supply was sweat. I'd experienced hot spells before, but this summer was bloody relentless. There was no respite from the blazing sun. When I hear 'The Boys Are Back in Town' by Thin Lizzy and 'Don't Go Breaking My Heart' by Elton John and Kiki Dee I'm immediately transported back to that hazy, lazy time. I can remember driving through the City of London and seeing office workers stripped down to bras, knickers and underpants occupying every patch of grass they could find, and even languishing spreadeagled on the steps of St Paul's Cathedral. When I hear the so-called weather experts of today frequently declaring that today, yesterday or tomorrow is the 'hottest day on record', I know they're rewriting history. The weather was sending people mad.

It certainly sent one person mad. It was in 1976 that I nearly witnessed a murder. Terry and I had a car showroom in Tooting, which also served as a meeting place for us chaps. I was driving there one day when I saw Old Bill all over the shop, sirens blaring, blue and white tape everywhere, and a sense of chaos. The action seemed to be on our forecourt. I turned the car around and made myself scarce. It turned out that two men, well known to me, had had a fight and one had died. 'Mad' Ronnie Fryer had stabbed Terry Marsh through the heart. Both were friends of Joey Pyle and, I thought, friends of each other.

Mad Ronnie (I apologise in advance for the disproportionate number of Ronnies in this book – they're everywhere) was well known for his volatility and had been sentenced to ten years in the 1960s after he shot at, but did not kill, the owner of the Cuckoo Club in Earl's Court. In that case his girlfriend stood trial with him because the gun was found in her handbag. She was cleared when the jury believed Ronnie's pleas that he'd put it in there without her knowledge.

Ronnie got his 'Mad' nickname because he did some of his bird in Broadmoor. I don't know why Joe had Ronnie wrapped round him. Me and Terry had fucked him off once from the car lot when he started putting his own motors for sale on our ground. He collected for Joe and carried out other odd jobs, but for me he was just too unpredictable and a disaster waiting to happen. He was known to wreak havoc in his wake, although he mainly behaved himself around Joey and his assets. I heard he knifed Terry over a barney over ten quid. Ten quid, for fuck's sake! A tragedy all round. Mad Ronnie went on the trot, perhaps not just from the police, as when he calmed down he'd have realised that Joey Pyle would not be too chuffed with him either.

It was also in the summer of 1976 I almost witnessed another murder not very far from the previous one. Mine. I was with Terry walking down Church Lane in Tooting and was semi-aware of passing a parked motor with a man in the driver's seat. In those days the only people that sat in cars that weren't running were perverts and undercover Old Bill. Now and then, that could be the same person. We kept walking. Didn't have a care in the world. I heard a door open behind me and then somebody call 'Oi!' Don't remember if the man added 'Ron' or not. He raised a gun and pointed it at me. The gun was barely visible, but my guess was it was a little 2.2-inch-barrelled revolver. When he shot, the jolt caused him to fire very low and he caught me in the foot. I hopped like I'd trod on a burning coal and fired back my far superior gun, a .38, and hit him where I'd aimed – in the torso. We walked off, me and Terry, around the corner and to his car, and when I looked back I could see my would-be assassin clutching his guts and staggering away. If he survived, I was pretty sure I'd given him a second tummy button.

Our first instinct was to drive to St George's Hospital, which was close, but we thought it best to go in the other direction. For all I knew I'd just murdered someone on a south London street. We eventually pulled over, and I removed my shoe and sock. Wiping away the blood, there was a flap of skin visible on the top of my foot. I lifted it up, and as I did the bullet tumbled out. We decided not to go to a hospital, and instead I went to a friendly house where a friendly doctor saw to me. Luckily, he said it was just a superficial wound.

To this day I genuinely have no idea who the man was. If he was a hitman, he wasn't a very good one. It must have been his first job as he was never going to kill me from that distance with that gun. It didn't have the range. Fine for putting one in somebody's nut – your breath on their neck – but not a target halfway down the road. It could have been a bloke with a personal grudge or even someone we'd sold a dodgy car to. Who knows? His aim was so bad, maybe he was trying to top Terry. I'll never know now. I was concerned for a few days, scanning the papers to see if anybody had snuffed it or for any accounts of gunfire, later racking my brains as to who it might be, and would they come back and try a bit harder? I wasn't too worried, but was a little more cautious afterwards. I never again sat in a restaurant with my back to the door, for example.

The average man or woman would have been shocked if they knew how many guns were being routinely carried around in London at that time. They were plentiful in our world. My mate Phil packed a .38 all the time. Little did the newsagent know when he served him his *Daily Mirror* and his packet of Trebor Mints each morning that his chatty regular customer had a loaded weapon in his inside jacket pocket.

Phil told me that when mugging first became a thing over here in the 1970s, he was walking home in the early hours of the morning in south London when four youths pulled up in a car and jumped out.

'Give us your money.'

One of them produced a knife. Phil stepped back took his revolver from the small of his back, where it was tucked in his waistband, and pointed the gun at them.

'No, you give me yours.'

Another time Phil's sister mentioned she was buying a second-hand car out of the paper. Phil had heard about a scam that some of the newly settled eastern Europeans were up to. They were advertising cheap non-existent cars in the evening paper, luring prospective buyers with cash to deserted places, taking the money and fucking off.

'I'll run you there,' said Phil.

Phil ended up by some garages on a council estate in Lewisham. A man beckoned him down an alleyway between the garages. Phil told his sister to wait in the car.

'Have you got the money?' demanded a gruff man in his thirties.

'Where's the car?'

'I need to see money first.'

'Well, I'm not going to pick the fucking car up and run off with it under my fucking arm, am I?' Phil growled.

The man shook his head.

'There's no car, is there?' Phil challenged.

The man smiled, so Phil pulled out his .38 and shot him in the legs twice. Getting back in the car he said, 'Car was crap, sis.'

'What were those bangs, Phil?'

'That was the car backfiring. Told you it was no good.'

'What about the screaming?'

'That was the bloke shouting at me because I told him the car was a wreck and he was trying to rip us off.'

To this day, Phil's sister has no idea what really happened. Or so Phil thinks.

8

SNATCHED

A busy weekend lay ahead of me. Among the criminal fraternity there was an informal network that operated like a sort of chamber of commerce, I guess. Firms from different regions of the country approached each other about potential work and sometimes swapped around graft. Now and then it made sense to carry out a job in a fresh area. We were given this opportunity up in Leeds in Yorkshire. There was inside information on a potential wages snatch at a clothing factory. We had plans of the building down to doors and windows, timings of cash deliveries, and the schedules and habits of the wages office.

Not so many people had bank accounts in those days, and even those that did were not paid invisibly by a credit to their account. Wages were handed out weekly in cash. At any one time cities and town were awash with bank notes travelling to factories, plants and offices, where these mountains of currency were counted up and placed in little brown envelopes and distributed to staff by clerks carrying trays. There were so many opportunities to relieve clerks and guards of loot. It was unbelievable, looking back.

Local robbers didn't fancy this Leeds work as they knew who the police would be coming to first. They were hot. Northern firms were less enthusiastic about using guns, and it was considered that this job required decisive and firm people management as it was a busy office environment. Our inside man, who didn't work for the clothing company but in the cash-delivery industry, estimated there would be around £100,000 of readies to be had. This was an enormous amount of money – about £1½m at today's prices. We were keen to take it on, happy to pay a commission should we be successful, but we already had a supermarket planned we wanted to get out the way. So, we decided to rob the supermarket on the Tuesday, travel up to Leeds on the Wednesday and carry out the wages snatch on the Thursday, which, it seemed, was payday up there.

The supermarket was in south-west London. We'd reccied the place first. The cash office was inside the shop but in a raised cabin up some stairs overlooking the whole floor. We knew that when Securicor arrived the safe would be open, waiting for the guards, so the collection would be rapid and smooth. We waited for the van to arrive, watched the two guards have a look left and right and enter the store, then followed them in. I rushed up behind them and fired into the ceiling.

'On the floor!' I shouted, and customers, staff and guards alike dropped to the ground.

'Keep still. Face the floor. Do as I say, and nobody will get hurt.'

To my dismay a couple of older women in buttoned-up macs and headscarves continued shopping, oblivious that they were in the middle of an armed robbery. Maybe their hearing aids weren't switched on. It could only happen in England. I shook my head and left them to it. Terry and Pat had leapt up the stairs, and were busy ladling out the contents of the safe into our cricket bag. I watched the floor carefully, especially the guards. Then, whack, a tin hit me in the chest. I looked around to see who'd thrown it, but everyone was still. Was it one of the old ladies from behind the soap-powder aisle? I looked down at the floor, and the offensive weapon was a tin of peas. Not even Farrows, just cheap, old, own-brand peas. Hurry up, boys, the peasants they are revolting.

Pat had emptied the safe into the bag and we walked out of the supermarket. We never ran. That would encourage people to chase. Smack of amateurism. Just when I stepped outside I caught the eye of a lorry driver sitting in his cab enjoying his elevenses. As he opened his mouth to sink his teeth into a doorstep cheese-and-pickle sandwich his eyes alighted on my stockinged face and the sawn-off in my hand. Like in a film, he slid down the seat to disappear himself from my line of vision. I smiled, but he wouldn't have been able to tell.

In the car Pat said it didn't feel like a lot of money, and for sure when we got to the pub afterwards and had a count-up, we were disappointed to see we only had a couple of thousand pounds. It was the 1970s, after all – a time when unemployment was on the rise, inflation was crippling us and the lights kept going out. A pound was worth a pound in the morning and 85p by 5 p.m. Never mind, we had a potential twenty-five grand *each* awaiting us in Leeds.

Terry, Pat, Colin and I travelled up the M1 in two cars that Pat had thieved the previous night. The motorway was still a novelty then. Driving through north London and seeing it open up for us was like travelling through a magic gate and a tarmac carpet unfurling before us to northern towns galore we'd only ever heard about or seen on the television or at the cinema. Hitchhikers clustered at the start of it, thumbing a lift, but we didn't think it a good idea to pick one up, especially with a couple of guns in the motor. Of course, we thought the north was all *Coronation Street*, coal mines, ferrets and brown ale, and in 1976 it probably was.

On arrival in Leeds, we plotted one car up for our getaway and then booked into a hotel. In the bar we went over our plan, soon turning in for an early night. In the morning we enjoyed a hearty breakfast and set off for the factory. We aimed to arrive at 10 a.m., when we were assured the wages would be there but not dished out yet. Parking outside, we donned our stockings and ski masks and ran down the side of the building to a staircase that took us up to the wages office on the fourth floor of this large factory. Not a good idea to take the lift. We picked up speed as we hiked up the stairs as the adrenaline began to pump furiously around our bodies. On the fourth floor there was a counter where staff came to collect their little brown wage packets, which were already being stood up in wooden trays. The counter was very small, and there was like a till and window that looked to be made of reinforced glass.

'Open the door!' I roared.

I kicked the door beside the till that was the entry to the department and banged on it, but it didn't budge. I then remembered that our insider had said the door was reinforced by metal, so I aimed the gun low and shot twice. Pandemonium ensued. The fucking door was made of plywood or some shit, and the thing practically disintegrated in front of me. Staff on the other side had been showered by wood splinters and pellets, and were screaming and shouting in pain, panic and shock. Others ran around the office, trying to escape. The alarm bells had been sounded and unbelievably other clueless workers were now appearing at the window to collect their wage packets. 'What on earth is going on?' I heard one man exclaim.

A bloke in overalls like a mechanic came at me with a huge spanner in his hand and tried to hit me. I rammed him in the chest with the butt of my sawn-off pump-action shotgun and he went down. He was lucky I didn't panic and shoot him. I looked at the others, and we knew it was on top and we had to scarper. It was a disaster for the staff, for us, for everyone. Terry headed down the stairs first, screaming at people to get out the way. I brought up the rear to make sure we all got out. We bundled into the car and screeched off towards the motorway.

Pulling our stockings off our faces, we didn't say much at first. We knew it was a bad day at the office and that we needed to take stock.

'They said the door was reinforced,' I eventually said.

'I know, Ron.'

I didn't know how many people had been hurt by my shots or if anyone had been killed. I doubted it. I'd shot low. Very low. And I didn't remember seeing blood or anyone looking like they were dead or dying. I hoped not, as it was not my intention to hurt anyone. It never was on a job. I was trying to gain rapid entry and scare somebody into opening the door. However, I'd be lying if I said that fear or remorse was uppermost in my mind. What was uppermost in my mind was getting away. Getting out of Leeds. Getting home.

The changeover to the second car went well, or so I thought, and soon we were out on that wide-open motorway, cruising along. We began to relax and talk over the debacle that had just taken place, and then we started to plan the next blag. Someone switched the radio on and picked up a local station.

'... raid this morning ... several shots have been fired ... four men ... armed and dangerous ... crazed gang ... do not approach ...'

Colin was looking into his rear mirror.

'There's nothing behind us,' he observed.

We all looked over our shoulders and through the back window. The road was clear. Eerie. Like an empty film set.

'There's nothing in front of us either,' said Terry.

The car went very quiet. Something wasn't right. Then up front we saw a long coach parked sideways across the lanes. In the distance now we could see some dark cars coming up behind, driving three abreast, lights flashing, and then up ahead we could see armed police crouching on the embankments, their Enfield rifles and telescopic sights trained on us. They were on both sides of the road and there were dozens of them. They were very distinctive in their caps and blue overalls.

'Don't lose your rag, Ron,' pleaded Terry, worried.

He knew – and the others knew – that this sort of thing enraged me, and I had a vicious temper. They feared that a shootout with the police would be an option I'd be considering. They thought I might aim to go down in a blaze of gory.

'That's the last thing I'm going to do, Tel,' I reassured him.

We pulled the car up and put our hands on our heads as the police approached us cautiously. We sat like statues, not wanting to give them any excuse to shoot us. I hadn't seen so much firepower since watching *Zulu* on TV on Christmas Day. The police took each of us out of the car one at a time and shoved us down to the floor, boot on the neck, hands behind our backs, and clamped us with old-fashioned handcuffs, not that pathetic tape they use today. Each one of us were put in a separate car and driven to Leeds nick.

We discovered later that they got ahead of us and on us due to a little boy. When we were changing into our second getaway vehicle this kid had seen us and apparently said, 'Mummy, don't those men look like bank robbers?'

He was very perceptive, this kid, because by now we'd changed into jackets and removed our masks. We thought we looked like respectable businessmen going to a conference. The kid was persistent and urged his mother to write our number plate down. This she reluctantly did, but she didn't report anything until she too heard on her car radio about the wages snatch – or nearly snatch – and she pulled over and phoned the police.

Undoubtedly this boy was a fan of *Police 5* – the predecessor of *Crimewatch* – which aired on television on a Sunday afternoon and was presented by a man with a comb-over and disproportionately large glasses called Shaw Taylor. In his five-minute slot before *The Big Match* he encouraged people to grass on their neighbours, their colleagues, their friends and even their families. Most of the crimes he used prime-time television to try and solve were unarmed robberies.

'Have you been offered cheap Bell's whisky recently?' he droned. 'Well, a lorryload of the tipple was hijacked last Wednesday near Dover. The driver is very shaken, but fortunately unhurt. The boxes are identifiable by the small red dot in the bottom left-hand corner of the label.'

This sort of nonsense. His catchphrase was 'Keep 'em peeled'. He was a menace, was Taylor.

I heard a story that in one episode he was displaying some paisley shirts with distinctive matching ties that had been nicked out of a warehouse in north London. Keep an eye out for them, urged Shaw as the programme closed. Next up was *The Big Match*, and the special guest was a well-known Arsenal and England footballer who turned up in the studio wearing a distinctive paisley shirt and matching tie. If it's not true, it should be.

Later it was alleged that the boy was put into protective custody because as an important witness his life was in danger. Again, a load of bollocks. It was a ruse by the police to horrify people and future jurors. Which it probably did, especially the poor kid, who we'd never have dreamed of laying a finger on. And how come his mother wasn't taken into protective custody too? She wrote the registration number down and would have seen us as well.

Have-a-go heroes were a thorn in the armed robber's side, the biggest single threat to the success of our endeavours. They could result in us leaving empty-handed or, worse still, us being deprived of our liberty for ten years or more. That's why I believed a decisive entrance, loud but clear shouting and a shot into the ceiling were necessary. The witnesses had to believe you meant business; any sign of weakness and hesitation could be pounced upon – witness the lady with the tin of peas (I'm assuming it was a lady) and the mechanic in Leeds with his large spanner. What was in their minds to challenge a likely desperate armed young man who'd already discharged a sawn-off shotgun in their presence? I have to say if a have-a-go merchant was going to seriously put us in danger I'd have shot them. Not to kill, but to wing. I'd have fired at the lower leg or foot, if that was going to be the difference between ten years and escaping. I hoped it would never happen.

One of the most famous have-a-go-hero cases was that of Alec de Antiquis back in 1947. Three lads – Charles Jenkins, Christopher Geraghty and Terence Rolt – went out armed to rob a jeweller's shop in Charlotte Street in the West End of London. This they did. During the robbery, they bashed the jeweller with a revolver gun and discharged a shot as they fled the scene. Alec de Antiquis was a father of six in his thirties and the owner of a small motorcycle repair shop. He was on his motorbike in Charlotte Street when he saw the men and quickly assessed the situation. He decided to ride the bike at them to impede their escape. Unfortunately for Alec (and them), one of the robbers shot him through the head and he died at the scene.

Public and media outrage followed. How could this happen on a West End street? The legendary Fabian of the Yard was assigned the case. Inspector Robert Fabian was one of the first celebrity coppers, played on TV by Bruce Seton in the 1950s and 60s. Years later I found out that Fabian lived around the corner from the Glyn Arms pub in Ewell. My grandparents or parents may have drunk with him unknowingly. With the help of another little boy who found the discarded gun, Fabian solved the case, and Jenkins and Geraghty were eventually hanged by Albert Pierrepoint in a double execution at Pentonville Prison. Terry Rolt avoided the noose on account of his age – he was only seventeen – and he was released from prison some ten years later.

The case inspired the 1950 film *The Blue Lamp*, where Dirk Bogarde shoots and kills old, uniformed copper Sergeant George Dixon. The movie was a huge success, which in turn spawned the long-running TV series *Dixon of Dock Green*, where despite being dead, good old dependable George Dixon managed another twenty years of police service. With a gammy leg too.

Back at Leeds police station we were interrogated singly for several sessions. There had been a few other jobs in the vicinity recently and the police fancied we were behind them too. We simply went, 'No comment', as you do. (I once heard a fellow inmate in prison say he came from a criminal family and his first words as a baby were 'no comment'. I thought that quite funny.) They said four people had been shot – who were all injured – and the mechanic who I'd clumped with the gun was also not too clever, they reckoned. I thought they were exaggerating but I wouldn't talk, and I knew the others wouldn't either. We were a good firm, with absolute confidence and trust in each other. After a couple of days we were taken to Leeds Magistrates' Court, where we were remanded in custody to Armley jail. Besides visiting, this was my first time inside a prison.

Armley looked like a dilapidated castle from the outside, and inside wasn't much better. Built in early Victorian times, it didn't appear like much modernisation had taken place since. What struck me most at first was the smell. It was an offensive, body-odour-type smell, mixed with shit. Didn't they wash up here? The oppressive heat didn't help either. Even the walls were sweating. The summer got hotter and hotter, and it seemed like it would never end. There was no respite, and we languished in our cells, gasping for water. It was the hardest bird I ever did. The screws gave us two jugs of water a day: one to wash with and one to drink. We were all so parched that both jugs had gone by midday, but the authorities reacted to the situation by locking us down. Confined to our cells. Then the men in their desperation went to the windows and cried out for more water when their pleas to the officers fell on deaf ears. It started off just one or two lone voices, and then we were all at it. Banging and shouting.

'Water! Water! Give us water!'

The good people of Armley began to gather around the perimeter of the jail. We were like dogs locked in a car on a sweltering day, and the public wanted us to be let out and watered. The general public are in favour of justice and law and order, but they're no fans of gratuitous cruelty.

'Give them water, you bastards,' they cried.

The screws were nervous. Prisoners were beginning to rebel across the country over poor conditions and staff brutality. Soon after this there was a three-day riot up the road in Hull Prison, where three-quarters of the place got smashed to bits. When we were finally let out of the cells, some of us went a bit berserk, lashing out. Angry, I instinctively rushed at the screw who opened my door, but he was built like a brick shithouse and he tossed me down the corridor like an Amazon parcel. By this time I was close to six feet tall myself and weighing fourteen or fifteen stone. I hit eighteen stone at one point, but this specimen dwarfed me. Things calmed down and a full-scale riot was averted.

I was in Armley for some months until our trial at Leeds Crown Court in October 1976. It was soon to be the year of the Queen's twenty-fifth jubilee, and I was about to get a lump of Her Majesty's pleasure. By this time I'd decided to plead guilty to the gun charges as there was no point in all four of us taking the rap for it, and after all it was me that did the shooting. It meant the other three would not get as much bird as they otherwise would have.

Vera Baird QC represented me. She was a young lady then but very competent. Vera went on to become a Labour MP, a government minister, the Solicitor General, and most recently the Victims' Commissioner for England and Wales. Also on the legal team was David Nathan, a young man at the time who'd go on to great things. He was the main QC on two of the trials resulting from the Brink's-Mat gold bullion robbery. David also defended members of the Arif family for armed robbery and snooker player Ronnie O'Sullivan's old man on a murder rap.

Neither Vera nor David could do very much for me as I'd pleaded guilty. The others went not guilty, but they couldn't do much for them either considering they were caught on the M1 red-handed with me, who was admitting guilt. The jury didn't deliberate for long, and as the judge handed down my sentence, at first I couldn't believe what I was hearing. He sentenced me to eight years for conspiracy to rob; twenty years for two counts of carrying a firearm with intent; ten years for robbery; ten years for aggravated burglary; and forty-eight years on four counts of assault with intent to rob. There were some grievous bodily harms in there too. The calculator in my head made that at least ninety-six years. Hopefully, though, I'd get a third off for good behaviour. That would bring it down to sixty-four years. I'd be out in the year 2040 at a sprightly ninety-four years of age, just in time to rob the Darby and Joan club. Fortunately, the judge added at the end as if an afterthought – 'to be served concurrently'. I ended up with a twelve-year term. Pat, Colin and Terry drew lesser sentences.

It was a lump. Twelve years. One hundred and forty-four months, six hundred weeks, four thousand, three hundred days. Whatever way you skinned it, that was a lot of porridge. The thought of not seeing Sadie grow up burned inside me. I wasn't happy at all, but it didn't break me. I figured I'd be out in nine or ten years, and I'd still be a relatively young man of forty years. I could resume my life then and get back to work. Besides, I'd been banged up with my demonic grandmother, Minnie Chatt, for fifteen years – whatever lay ahead couldn't be worse than that. You had to think that way or you'd sink into a depressive swamp you might never crawl out of.

This was before they'd started categorising prisoners as Category A, B and C, etc. I was 'on the book' – a forerunner of the Cat A – which meant in practice I carried a little book around with my name in it that had to be signed by an officer whenever I moved around the prison. It was a rigmarole. What it meant was that we who had the book were thought to be at high risk of escaping – that we had the wherewithal, the resources and the contacts to break out of jail. It crossed my mind that I should have a go if it meant I'd be recaptured and get a nick closer to home, which would be better for everyone, but knowing the system they would then send me to Barlinnie or Devil's Island or somewhere.

My sentence continued at Armley jail. Carol and Jackie – separately, of course – would trek all that way to visit me and sometimes bring Sadie. I loved seeing them. They'd make that long, long rail journey to Leeds, yet the prison authorities would never give us more than fifteen minutes together. I went to see the governor and explained about how they had to travel two hundred miles on trains and buses, and then the visits were so short. Could we have extra time? The governor was surprisingly sympathetic and promised to sort something out. I was incredibly grateful.

At the next visit we were just getting into it when the warder said, 'Come on, Field, your time's up.'

'Hang on,' I protested, 'the governor has said we're allowed some extra time.'

'You've had it, old son,' replied the warder. 'You've had twenty minutes. Five minutes extra. Now, get a move on.'

Five minutes? Bastards. It was subtle mental mind games they liked to play. They were at it all the time.

Later in that first year inside I got word from Joe Pyle via my solicitor that he'd a ruse to get us back down to London. Mad Ronnie Fryer had had enough of being on the run and had given himself up to the police. A trial would ensue. Joe thought it might be a good idea if me and Terry said we'd witnessed something, in which case we'd be moved down to London, for the trial at least. Before we had time to kick this idea around we got word that Ronnie Fryer had done away with himself in Brixton jail. Or that was the story. So that was that.

I was moved to Walton Prison in Liverpool. No particular reason, they just liked to shuffle prisoners around the country so they didn't become too embedded, too familiar with their surroundings, too comfortable. It was another old Victorian jail that had seen better days. They said that during the bombing of Liverpool in the Second World War the nick took a direct hit, killing twenty people. If that wasn't bad enough, one of the bodies wasn't recovered until eleven years later, when the prison workers finally cleared the last of the debris. We had our own screws come with us to Walton as we were still the equivalent of Cat A prisoners. The Liverpool screws didn't like us and resented our special treatment. I was in there about nine months.

Then they ghosted me to HMP Strangeways, and a more aptly named prison you'll never find. Ghosting was the practice touched on above where the screws would come and wake you in the early hours of the morning, get you to collect up your belongings and you were gone into the still of the night to another prison, where you'd have to start all over again. It was designed to break you, to exert their power over you. And for many young and delicate prisoners it did. It was a cruel practice that made no sense. They argued it was a necessary control mechanism for difficult prisoners. But surely the idea is to make inmates less difficult, not more? I wasn't at Strangeways long, but for enough time to join in a riot over conditions, slap a screw and get a few days in solitary as a result. I was getting a reputation as a rebellious and dangerous prisoner.

Strangeways properly exploded some thirteen years later, when the endless brutality from the screws and the dire conditions drove the residents to riot, this time taking the prison over and burning much of it down. They took to the roof for a protest that lasted nearly a month. When the officers withdrew at the start of the riot, many of the prisoners headed for the medicine stocks while others hunted down the nonces and one was killed. That riot, and a raft of others around the country, ultimately led to the Woolf Report, which concluded that the conditions at Strangeways were intolerable and led to significant changes in the prison system.

Eventually common sense prevailed for me, and I was told I was being moved closer to home, to HMP Parkhurst on the Isle of Wight, where an unexpected reception committee awaited me.

9

KRAY DAYS

In the canary, as we called the caged compartment in prison vans, I was handcuffed one arm to the floor and the other up high to a bar, making me look like I was a kid imitating a fighter plane listing to one side. There were four screws, including the driver, minding me. They drove us from prison to prison in those days in bright yellow vans, which I always thought was barking mad as it marked us out so clearly. Far lesser criminals than me have been sprung on journeys from prison to prison or court to prison. Such escapades can end in somebody getting hurt. To make doubly sure everyone knew a dangerous man was being transported they had the siren on all the time, which was all right for them as they were wearing ear defenders.

At Portsmouth there were urgent conversations between the warders and the ferry staff, who were saying the weather conditions were too bad and they shouldn't sail.

'We can't take him back,' the warders insisted.

So, against somebody's better judgement, an almost empty ferry set off with me tethered in the back of the van while my captors disappeared off somewhere. My guess is the bar. I reminded them that under maritime law, prisoners are not meant to be tethered when the boat is sailing.

'Tough,' grunted one.

It was not as if I could have gone anywhere. I only wanted a pint too, and to check out the duty free.

At about 2 a.m. we approached the forbidding gates of Parkhurst Prison on the outskirts of Newport on the Isle of Wight. They opened, and we drove into a forecourt from where I was escorted into the reception area.

'You must be very important, Mr Field,' said the booking-in officer, looking down at the clipboard with my paperwork attached.

'I don't think so, guvnor. Why do you say that?'

'Because there are two gentlemen here to see you.'

'Really?'

I didn't know what to expect. A couple of detectives from the Metropolitan Police here to lay some new charges on me over some long-forgotten blag? The heads of the escape committee already?

'Hello, Ronnie. I'm Reg Kray and this is my brother Ron.'

As if I didn't know who they were. The twins stood up from where they'd been sitting patiently while I was processed and enthusiastically shook my hand.

'Welcome to Parkhurst,' smiled Ron.

They then proceeded to shower me with gifts: tobacco, sugar, tea, coffee, biscuits and chocolate.

'Thanks a lot, Reg. Ron. This is really thoughtful of you. Very kind indeed.'

'No problem, Ronnie. Any friend of Joe's is a friend of ours,' said Reg. 'Now settle in. Get some kip and we'll have a good old chinwag in the morning over a cup of tea.'

Reg nodded over to the officer as if to say, 'OK, you can carry on now', and I was led to my cell.

I was elated at my VIP welcome, at the friendship the twins had extended to me and about the gifts, which mean so much inside. I'd never met Ron or Reg before, and they looked well, although leaner, gaunter and a touch greyer than they did in all the photographs from around the time of their trial nearly a decade earlier. Ron, especially. Prison life does that. Obviously, they were in prison clothes, not the pin-striped suits and silk ties I was used to seeing them wearing in the papers. I particularly liked that about the Krays, that they never allowed themselves to be photographed dressed in an old T-shirt or jeans. They were always smart, and both carried a tailored suit so well. That brief exchange in the reception area, and the body language between them and the screws, gave me a first inkling of who the real guvnors were in this jail.

The twins continued to make a fuss of me, introducing me to all the inhabitants of C Wing (where Reg lived) and D Wing as a good friend, and as promised we drank tea together the next day, they showed me around their own separate cells and took me to visit others in their cells. They seemed to come and go almost as they pleased, with courteous exchanges with the officers as they passed each other. I was impressed. Danny Allpress and a few of the boys from the Wembley armed robbery mob were in too, minus Bertie Smalls, obviously. Billy was another armed robber I was introduced to, who I grew to like a lot. He'd had the misfortune of having had the front of his foot blown off when his fellow blagger's gun accidentally fired while they were piling into the getaway car.

The warders were more like butlers around the twins than captors. There was talk that some officers did well financially by accommodating their wishes. That's how it seemed to me on first impressions. It reminded me of a film I saw as a kid, *Two-Way Stretch*, which starred Peter Sellers and Bernard Cribbins as cons and Lionel Jeffries as the prison officer. I wouldn't be surprised if this film was the inspiration for the sitcom *Porridge*. The line in the film that came to mind was when Lionel Jeffries approaches Sellers and Cribbins's cell door and knocks on it ever so gently.

'Come in, it's not locked,' shouts Sellers.

The history of Parkhurst is fascinating. The jail was originally constructed in Newport as a military hospital and children's asylum. In 1838 it became a prison for the first time, housing young male offenders. A newspaper of the time reported on the aspirations of Parkhurst's founders:

The prison, when fully arranged, will receive 500 criminals, who are to be taught trades, as well as reading, writing and useful knowledge; their religious and moral education to be particularly attended to during their period of confinement. Instead of being turned adrift again on the world at the expiration of their sentence, they will be enabled by these blessings to become sober and steady members of the commonwealth.

Not sure I came across much religious and moral education in my time doing time on the island, but 'commonwealth' is the key word there – even though it lacked its current meaning at the time – as many of those early young men and boys were transported to Australia and New Zealand to complete their penal servitude in a government-sponsored Victorian version of human trafficking. Queen Victoria herself visited Parkhurst, where the women prisoners (who were now being housed there) refused to welcome her by singing the national anthem as instructed, and when she departed they rioted over poor conditions. In 1869, just after this regal visit, the prison reverted to being male only.

Steinie Morrison, a Russian man living in England, was a famous former inmate. A criminal known for organising jewellery heists and armed robberies, he was convicted of murdering Leon Beron on Clapham Common in 1911. Some said he was a political activist and had connections to the Sydney Street siege of 1911. The letter 'S' was apparently carved into Beron's body, which prompted all sorts of theories of espionage, dodgy foreigners and secret societies. Morrison always protested his innocence, and died in Parkhurst in 1921 while on hunger strike for his cause.

Ruby Sparks, a smash-and-grab specialist in his early days and a well-known villain and burglar, did time in Parkhurst too. He'd earlier led a riot at Dartmoor Prison over conditions and poor treatment, and he's said to be the only man to have escaped from both Strangeways and Dartmoor prisons. Also in trouble for leading a riot, this time in Parkhurst, was Frankie Fraser in 1970. In the 1970s Frank was Britain's most famous rebellious prisoner, a mantle that Charlie Bronson would later inherit. The conditions and brutality in the Isle of Wight prisons of Parkhurst, Camp Hill and Albany that Frank and his fellow inmates rebelled against hadn't changed much by the time of my arrival.

Also sharing our island bang-up during my time was John Duddy, one of the men convicted alongside Harry Roberts of killing three unarmed policemen in Shepherd's Bush in 1966. I met him but didn't know him well. He kept himself to himself and was doing a bricklaying course when we crossed paths. He'd done a lot of bird and died in Maidstone nick in 1981, just before he was due for release. His co-defendants did eventually get freed, John Witney in 1991 becoming the first police killer ever to be released from prison, although he was murdered by his flatmate in 1999. Harry Roberts, once Britain's most wanted man when he had it on his toes following the triple shooting, got freed in 2014 after serving forty-eight years. For a period in 1966, Harry's mug shot was beamed into people's homes via their black-and-white television sets even more often than Sean Connery. Football grounds around the country resounded to the chant of 'Harry Roberts is our friend, is our friend, Harry Roberts is our friend, he kills coppers'. No wonder football supporters aren't high on policemen's Christmas card list.

Graham Young, the poisoner, was another sharing porridge with us on the island. Well, I was careful not to share any actual porridge with him, because Graham had a habit of lacing drinks and food he prepared for family, friends and colleagues with lethal substances. He'd been sent to Broadmoor as a youth after poisoning his father, stepmother and sister, only to be let out to kill some work colleagues a few years later by lacing their drinks. Needless to say, Graham was kept well away from the tea urn.

One afternoon we'd run low on powdered milk, tea and coffee, so me and a few of the lads had an idea (making and drinking tea and coffee take up a disproportionate amount of your time when there's fuck-all else to do). I pulled a warder up and said, 'Guvnor, none of my business, I know, but I saw that Graham Young coming out of your tearoom earlier.'

'What! Thanks, Ronnie.'

And as I thought, loose teabags and opened jars of coffee, powdered milk and sugar were gathered up and dumped into the waste bin. When the coast was clear, I nipped in and retrieved the lot. Happy days.

It was always thought – by us – that Graham managed to poison people in Parkhurst, although I can't recall any specific instances. Anyone that had an upset stomach – con or screw – always wondered whether Graham had been able to get near his grub, and when he was found dead in his cell years after I'd left, there were rumours he might have poisoned himself or even that a screw gave him some of his own medicine.

Peter Sutcliffe, the cowardly nonce, came to Parkhurst. He was the brute who stalked the backstreets of Leeds and beyond, mercilessly battering to death defenceless women with a hammer. The media dubbed him the 'Yorkshire Ripper', which he probably got off on, but he was living here in a closed society where plenty of people wanted to kill or maim him.

The threat to him was so real that he was kept alone in his unit on C Wing, and they built a small exercise yard at the back of his cell for him alone. We couldn't get near that exercise yard, but a friend of mine's cell overlooked it. Over time, this friend painstakingly made a lethal bow and arrow, and was planning to shoot Sutcliffe in the neck or face – but a routine spin of his cell put a stop to that. Shame. After the do-it-yourself Robin Hood kit was discovered, a prisoner called James Costello stuck a broken coffee jar in Sutcliffe's face. The authorities now realised that eventually somebody would surely top him in Parkhurst, so he was moved to Broadmoor, where violent tendencies were suppressed by strong drugs. Life might have been worse there for him, though, what with a grinning Jimmy Savile visiting him every other week.

Another notorious Peter – Peter Samuel Cook, aka the Cambridge Rapist – was also on our wing. Convicted of several rapes of university students in the mid-1970s, for a

Mum at the jellied eels stall
outside the Red Lion in Cheam
around 1960.

Dad in uniform. Private Walker from
Dad's Army could have been
modelled on him.

Billy, Dalla and Pat around 1944.

My oldest sister, dear Pat, in 1949.

Me (left), Ciss and friend Graham in the back garden of Malden Road circa 1956.

Late 1950s, I already knew my way around a gun.

My wedding day, 1964, with my brother Ted (right), who was my best man.

The chaps at my wedding, 1964. The Beatles are all the rage, but we remain Teds.

Happy days with
Charlie Kray and Mrs
Kate Kray.

At Ron Kray's wedding to
Kate Howard in 1989.

Roy Shaw claims the first
dance with Mrs Kray.
Cornish Mick, me and
Joey Pyle look on.

Passing some dosh to Craig Shergold. He ended up receiving around 350 million cards wishing him well.

With Jimmy White, visiting Joey Pyle in Parkhurst.

Ron Kray's funeral in 1995.
I am at the front, to the left of the gentleman in dark glasses.

Cornish, Bobby Gould and me in 1999.

Blackie Saxton, a very
good friend and partner.

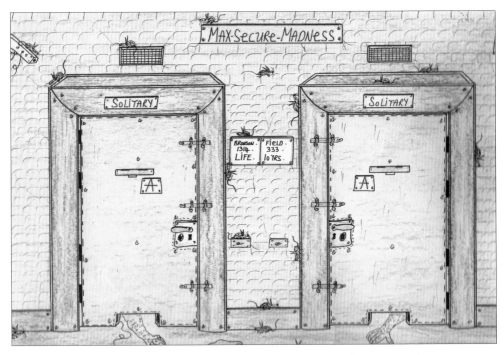

Charlie Bronson gifted me several of his unique drawings – this
one recalls our days in isolation.

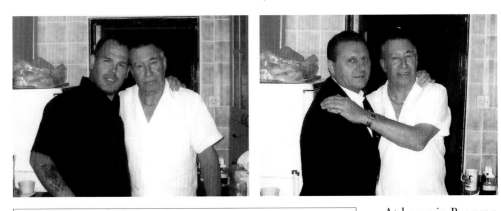

At home in Bronson
Road with great
friends Andy and Jon.

To

Ron
–

Your Val Reg Kray.

Just another Christmas greeting
Of the old familiar kind,
But it brings the warmest wishes
You could ever hope to find.

Merry Christmas
and a Happy New Year

I miss my annual
Christmas card from
Reg Kray.

Two of the best:
Freddie Foreman and
Joey Pyle.

Me and Fred with my
daughter Sadie.

Joe Pyle's funeral in 2007,
with Freddie Foreman
and Roy Shaw.

With my dear sisters again at the other end of our lives.

Catching up with Chris Lambrianou (top right), Kenny Noye (above) and the late Dave Courtney (left) in 2023.

while the university city lived in fear as Cook prowled at night in a leather mask with a zip for his mouth, holes for his eyes and the word RAPIST scrawled on it. Cook was unusual for a rapist inasmuch as he refused to go on the numbers. This meant that he didn't opt for the application of Rule 43, which would have put him – for his own protection – on the wing where child molesters and rapists were kept separate from other prisoners who were likely to attack them, and kill them if they could. For example, Donald Neilson, the bloke they called the 'Black Panther', was also in Parkhurst while I was there, but I never saw him as he opted to stay in segregation. Neilson was big news for a while when he kidnapped Lesley Whittle, the heir to a coach company fortune, and held her way down in a drain shaft shivering on a ledge with a noose around her neck deep in the Black Country somewhere. He ended up killing the poor girl.

Cook used to get beat up at first, but he still chose to remain with us, and after a while as far as I know he was left untouched. He'd done time as a younger man, being in and out of borstal and prison for burglary offences. At some point when entering victims' houses his mind turned to rape and sexual assault. He was known to escape from the scene of crimes riding a bike, dressed in women's clothing and wearing a blonde wig. Cookie, as many of us called him, kept himself to himself, making top-notch models of caravans and vehicles from matches, and although there was not a lot of mixing, his bottle in choosing to stay on the wing was acknowledged. The warders told us he was a hermaphrodite, which I understand means he possessed both male and female sexual organs, and they reckoned he had a tiny micro-penis. I don't know if any of that was true, but we believed it at the time, and we wondered in that case how he managed to rape anyone. Cook died in Winchester Prison in 2004.

We had a man on our wing who came to us from Albany Prison, just down the road from us in Newport. He weighed about seven stone, dressed as a woman and called himself Mary. Despite his size he'd stabbed up people in Albany, so he was treated with some caution and left to his own devices. The thought of him being moved to a women's prison fills me with dread. It couldn't happen then and there were good reasons why.

The incarcerated population were more tolerant of homosexuality than the population on the outside were in those days. What consenting adults do in privacy has never been my concern. The only people who shared cells in Parkhurst in my memory were two or three gay couples. We called that part of the wing the 'married quarters'. I knew well a couple of armed robbers who became what we called 'prison poofs'. This was when a con had a homosexual relationship inside but reverted to his heterosexual ways on the outside.

There were only 198 prisoners in the whole jail at this time, although I believe Parkhurst could have held 800 inmates. With us were several IRA men. Some of the Old Bailey and alleged Birmingham bombers were there, along with a couple of UDA men. The IRA inmates largely only mixed with one another, but if trouble blew up with the guards they'd be the first in – and there was no doubt whose side they were on. Sometimes the IRA would say there was something big going to happen the next day, and it did. One of those occasions was before Lord Mountbatten, members of his family and an Irish boy were blown up by an IRA bomb planted on his boat in County Sligo. Could have been a lucky call, but I don't think so.

One day I walked past a cell and a group of IRA men were in there sitting quietly, listening intently to one of their men who was standing in front of a blackboard teaching them.

'What's going on there?' I asked a screw.

'Bomb-making classes,' he said.

'Oh, is that all?' I commented sarcastically.

Ron Kray would summon me and Reg over for tea and chats. The brothers were both polite and generous to a fault – standing up when people came into the room, enquiring after our families, checking if we had enough baccy, calling the tea boy over to fill our cups. We'd talk about the past, theirs normally, and what was going on in the outside world. Ron would read letters aloud he'd received from 'fans' and the brothers would discuss business. They always stressed how much they liked and respected Joey Pyle, and spoke in similar glowing terms of Freddie Foreman, the legendary south London villain who they'd befriended in the 1960s and was sentenced alongside them.

'We never took money from them,' Reg once commented.

No, you didn't, I thought. *Because neither of them would ever have paid you.* But I kept that to myself.

Both brothers loved to reminisce about the 'old days' – some stories I'd heard before, and some I hadn't. I could only listen, as I wasn't around in the period they talked about; too young to know these 1950s and early 1960s faces and hard men they'd be describing. There wasn't anyone who was anyone they hadn't met. The names of film stars, TV people and high-profile boxers tripped off their tongues.

Reg used to invite me to his cell for drinks in the evening. I soon learned that some prisoners ordered alcohol from screws, who'd smuggle it in. On poor wages, some officers were easily corrupted by inmates paying £100 for a bottle of vodka, the financial transaction taking place on the outside at arm's length. One evening we were drinking when the prison officer opened the cell door fully.

'Come on, Field, time to get back to your own cell,' he ordered.

I got up to go.

'Sit down, Ronnie,' said Reg firmly. 'He hasn't finished his drink.' This to the screw.

The screw withdrew timidly, and I finally returned to my cell voluntarily about an hour later. Nobody else in the jail or the whole prison system had such clout. It was surreal. Sometimes, after a good drink in another inmate's cell, some of the more exuberant of us would return to our cells bouncing, spinning and doing handstands in the suicide net on the way. The suicide net was apparently there to stop us throwing ourselves off the balconies, but the main reason was to prevent us throwing furniture and improvised missiles down on to the screws below.

Ron scared me, I do admit, although Joe once said that Reg was the more dangerous brother because he was good at concealing his mood and not giving away any violent intention until it was too late. With Ron, he couldn't hide his feelings. If he started getting the needle with someone he'd growl, 'Fuck off, you're getting on my nerves.'

And if you had any sense you'd fuck off. Reg, on the other hand, might pull you close, seemingly in a hug, and then do you one way or another. That's what Joe said.

Ron liked to talk, and he'd sometimes fix his stare on me and say, 'Know what I mean, Ronnie?'

He was checking I was listening. I dared not drift off and let my attention stray. Sometimes his lower leg would tremble and he'd place his hand on his knee firmly to stop it. A silent battle between upper limb and lower limb then ensued. This was a sign that he was becoming vexed, or even angry. Reg and I would look at one another, and Reg would diplomatically end the meet, or Ron would stand up and say, 'Forgive me, gentlemen. I need to go now.'

He knew when his black moods were descending, and he knew best how to deal with them. But not always.

One afternoon we were sitting in the lounge area of the hospital wing where Ron now lived, drinking tea and half-heartedly watching television. Me, Reg, Ron and a couple of other prisoners – one was a bloke called Billy, who the twins liked. A young red band – an inmate who the authorities trusted – was charged with the job of refilling our cups. He'd walk around with his stainless-steel bucket, politely asking if we wanted refilling. It was his first day on this job, Ron told us. It was all very civilised.

The lad refilled us one by one and got to Ron. He nodded, the boy poured and walked off to the next group. Ron glared into his mug and then jumped up, shouted something, and snatched the urn from the lad and poured the scalding water over his head. The warders pulled Ron away and ushered the traumatised trusty out of the room.

'What did you do that for, Ron?' asked Reg, shocked and cross.

'He was taking the piss out of me.'

'How was he taking the piss out of you, Ron?'

'He only poured me half a cup, Reg.'

'But you only have a half a cup, Ron.'

'Yeah, but he doesn't know that, does he? He's new, Reg. He was trying to mug me over.'

'He wasn't, Ron. Don't you think they'd have told him you only have half a cup?'

That hadn't occurred to Ron, I don't think. I was keeping out of it. Ron stood up and left the room before he was escorted away. It wasn't long after this that he was transferred to Broadmoor, the high-security psychiatric hospital in Crowthorne, Berkshire, and I wouldn't see him again until he was a patient, and I was a visitor.

10

BANG-UP BLUES

Trouble was brewing all over in Parkhurst. There was a lot of madness about, and that was just the warders. Conditions were bad, the food was awful and getting worse, and prison staff were taking industrial action over staff shortages and pay, making things difficult for us. Sometimes things blew. A prisoner was stabbed to death in the dining area because he ate another man's bowl of Corn Flakes one morning. The ridiculous thing was that the prisoner never ate his allotted Corn Flakes, so the man that died never thought he was taking a liberty. What a thing to lose your life over. Another time a prisoner was soaking in a metal bath when an inmate came in, leant over the side and harpooned him with a sharpened broom handle through the belly. This was a row over tobacco, of which there were plenty.

I was a troublesome prisoner. I was still a young man full of testosterone with a chip the size of a breeze block on my shoulder against authority and the system. Without exception in those early days, I detested the screws. One day I complained about something, and a lairy screw came over and poked me. I fucking hate that. I'd rather be chinned than poked in the chest. It's like someone saying they're better than you. Arrogance. The red mist descended, I whacked him as hard as I could on the jaw, his legs buckled and he went down. I was grabbed by a bunch of screws and taken down into the punishment block – the chokey – and a solitary cell. I knew exactly what punishment was coming.

An hour later, four of them turned up at my door and rushed me. I fought back, but I didn't stand a chance, taking the baton blows, the kicks, punches, headlocks and head-butts as best I could. Four of them, though! Who did they think I was? Fucking Batman? This ritual played out two or three times in Parkhurst, but when they realised I wouldn't stand for any bullying and could take what they dished out, the lines were drawn. They were less aggressive to me.

Another reason I calmed down was that after one of these bust-ups between me and the screws, I was sent to see Dr Cooper, the prison psychiatrist. He questioned and probed me, trying to find a peg to hang my anger on, but I didn't say too much. Then he said he wondered if I'd be more suited to a different environment.

'We'll give it a couple of months, but if you don't calm down we'll have to look at transferring you to somewhere you can get help for your anger and be treated.'

'Fuck off! I'm not mad!' I shouted, gripping the chair tightly and just stopping myself from leaping across the desk.

'See what I mean,' the doctor said.

I didn't like the way the conversation was going. I was shocked and started to wise up, assuring him of my sanity and vowing to simmer down.

A few days later a good screw came to my cell. Although I forget his name, he was a truly decent man, and he asked me, 'You don't smoke puff, do you, Ronnie?'

'No, not my bag, guv.'

'You should give it a try. I think it might help you in here. Level you out a bit.'

'I don't do drugs at all. Never even taken a purple heart.'

'I think you'll benefit from a puff now and then.'

He went on to tell me that he'd heard whispers that 'they' had been talking about sending me to Broadmoor. I could now see exactly what Dr Cooper had in mind.

'I'm not mad,' I protested.

'They're beginning to think you are, Ronnie. That's the problem.'

'Fucking hell.'

'Give it a try,' he said.

Then he sat down and showed me how to roll a joint. He took a bit of gear from his breast pocket. He said it was Black Moroccan, removed the cellophane and proceeded to burn it with a lighter. Between forefinger and thumb he crumbled the dope on top of a line of tobacco he'd laid out on some fag papers, then stuck them together with a flick of his tongue.

'Smoke it later. When you feel stressed,' he said.

It was an act of kindness, and I'd use puff to help me through for the rest of my prison life. I'll always be grateful to that screw for caring and tipping me the wink about what the doctor and the governor might have been planning. I ran into him years later when I was in Belmarsh on the single A Wing. He was one of two screws who carried out a routine spin of my cell.

'You shouldn't have this, Ronnie,' he said, holding up a bit of gear and shaking his head. I didn't hear any more so, again, he did me a right favour.

I heard later that Dr Cooper was found wandering around Parkhurst Forest naked. It could have been a prison myth, but it wouldn't surprise me. The job could well have sent him mad. Parkhurst was a drop-off for Broadmoor and he spent all his time dealing with dangerous psychopaths, so what do you expect? It wouldn't be surprising if the man responsible for nutting people off went nuts himself.

The turning point in warder and inmate relations was when the prison staff went on strike one time. A big job to repair the antiquated Victorian drain network was under way, and even the labouring men who were working on this walked out. Out in the courtyard between C Wing, D Wing and the hospital wing, an entrance to the underground drains was left open. Before we knew it there were rats everywhere. We were used to a few mice and the odd cockroach, but this was like an invasion. Big black fuckers, I swear. Never seen anything like it. There was a book out at the time – *The Rats* by James Herbert – check out the cover of that. Enormous, horrifying bastards, like rabid cats. They got inside the blocks, and you'd hear them at night squealing and scampering around the corridors. It was a major infestation, and nothing was being done about it. In the courtyard they scuttled back and forth without a care in the world, running, jumping and tumbling over each other in their unbridled joy, like they were goading us. It was reminiscent of a Hammer horror film. When we found evidence of their visits in the dining area we snapped. The shit literally had hit the porridge.

We rioted, smashing up chairs and attacking the warders, who sensibly retreated. Soon we'd gained control of A Wing, D Wing and the yard. We thought about scaling the walls and breaking out, but a mass escape would inevitably fail – we were on an island, after all. I thought it was a silly idea but joined in anyway. Never a party pooper, me. Later, we calmed down and went on hunger strike. We were well within our rights, and the IRA boys knew all about the power of hunger striking. Prison authorities and governments don't like it, as peaceful but powerful protest confuses them. Each day we'd queue up as usual at the serving hatch, take our meals, walk across the room and slide the food off our plates into the bins. Don't know if we imagined it, but the food they sent in seemed to be of better quality – this was to tempt us to break the strike, we believed.

We kept it up for four days, at which point the governor opened up negotiations. The warders came back to work, presumably having got a settlement themselves, and with no acknowledgement our action had helped their cause. That first evening when the hunger strike was called off they sent in a vat full of hot, steaming porridge. After four days no food has ever tasted so good or been so roundly appreciated. All the grub then got better, the drains were closed and other conditions began to slowly improve. So, maybe the rats did us a favour.

Next up, and the last stop before my eventual release, was Maidstone jail in Kent. It was a B and C Category nick where us prisoners who'd served long sentences were prepared for liberty. I got a job in the gardens, which I loved. I worked closely with an officer called Nick Clark, who was an old Dartmoor screw in charge of the gardens, and another called Sammy, both of them fair men. I loved being outside, working with the plants and the soil. Nick was a diamond who gave much more to others than he ever took.

Charlie Bronson, later to be dubbed Britain's 'most dangerous prisoner' on account of a catalogue of tear-ups with officers, inmates and items of furniture, was also in the gardens working on the allotments. He'd already changed his name to that of the Hollywood actor famous for playing hard but silent types in films such as *The Great Escape* and *Death Wish*. If our Charlie had been forensic about the name change he should have called himself Charles Buchinsky, as that was his hero actor's real name. Or Charlie could have offered Charles a swap and offered up his own real name – Michael Peterson – in exchange.

I'd get to know Charlie much better later, when Joe Pyle promoted him briefly as an unlicensed fighter, and even better later again when Hollywood came knocking. It was while working in the gardens that Charlie was stabbed one day. I wasn't there so can't comment on what happened.

One afternoon Nick approached me in the allotments as I was bedding in some flowers. 'Ronnie,' he said, 'do you fancy going outside the nick and cutting the lawns at the warders' quarters?'

'I'll have some of that, Nick.'

'You must give me your word, though. Your word you'll not try and escape. If you do, my credibility will be shot to shreds.'

'You have my word, Nick,' I replied as we firmly shook hands.

And I meant it. My word is important. If I say I'm going to do something, I'll do it, whether it's good or bad. People who know me will tell you that.

A couple of weeks later Nick pulled me to one side again. 'Fancy a Sunday out, Ronnie? The deputy governor needs his garden attended to. Would you like to do it?'

'I'd enjoy that, guvnor.'

'No escaping?'

'You have my word. I told you.'

'Yes, Ronnie.'

The deputy governor was called Tony French and he lived in a substantial house not too far from the prison. It was a Sunday, and I grafted from early morning to mid-afternoon. The garden was in a state and hadn't been touched for some time. I thought I might find a Japanese soldier in the undergrowth. Tony came into the garden as the light started to dim.

'How are you doing, Ronnie?'

'Good, thank you, Guvnor.'

'I hope you're hungry, because Sunday dinner is being served inside.'

I followed Tony into the house and sat with him in front of my first lovingly made roast in a decade. Tony offered me a can of beer, which I accepted, and after dinner we went into a room where he and I sat alone.

'Do you drink spirits?' he asked.

'Not so much recently,' I smiled. (That was a lie. I'd not long ago enjoyed a couple of evenings in Freddie Foreman's cell sharing vodka the screws supplied us for a ton a bottle. Vodka, puff and good company – you can't beat it.)

Tony poured me a generous tumbler of Scotch. We talked about my sentence, my release and the riots in Parkhurst.

'You know if you lot had gone over the wall that day, armed police were on the other side under orders to shoot you? The government wouldn't have allowed that. There was no way they were going to let you lot stream across the island hijacking cars and sailing off in boats like it was Dunkirk in reverse. It could have brought the government down.'

I didn't know that, and I said it was a good job we didn't try then.

Tony refilled me a couple of times, and as I was not that used to alcohol I quickly felt a bit steamed. We had a long chat, with Tony telling me about his life and me telling him about mine. He seemed genuinely interested. He was an unusual prison governor and I wished there were more like him in the prison service.

'Come on,' he eventually smiled. 'Let's get you back to the nick or we'll both fall asleep.'

Tony escorted me back to the jail personally. To ensure the warders didn't clock I was a bit pissed, he walked me right back to my cell.

'Good night, Ronnie. Thank you for your hard work and I must say I've enjoyed your company today.'

'The feeling is mutual, Guvnor.'

This man's extraordinary kindness and trust have stayed with me. After that I did half a dozen screws' houses. Their gardens, that is. Tony had set me up for a much more pleasant and rewarding bit of time.

Later one of the senior screws asked me if I'd like to be a 'listener' for other prisoners in distress. A listener would sit in the cell with inmates who were suffering depression or were even suicidal and hear their pain and talk things through. I didn't consider myself right for such responsibility as I wasn't the most empathetic person in the nick, so I declined the offer. Nevertheless, now and then a screw would ask me informally to go and sit with someone or other they were concerned about, and I did it. Whether it helped, I don't know, but I do have a feeling it was Tony that put me up for that one. Tony went on to rise very high in the criminal justice system, and deservedly so.

One tragic case I remember was a very good armed robber who was coming to the end of his sentence, having served around eighteen years. Who knows why, but his wife or partner ended their relationship before his release, and he went off and killed himself. He may have been in turmoil about going back into society after all that time, but his wife finishing with him at the same time was perhaps unbearable.

Towards the end of my sentence I rediscovered the joy of reading. I'd taken over running the book club in Parkhurst from Bruce Reynolds, the Great Train Robber, but hadn't done a great deal of reading there. In Maidstone we were allowed one visit to the library a month, when we could take away three books. The problem was I'd read these in as many days. I'd hunt around the wing looking for people to swap with, but I was always book-hungry. Why they couldn't give us unlimited access, I don't know. It would have kept a lot of people a lot quieter. I read Mickey Spillane and loved his character Mike Hammer, a private investigator who fought crime and was unafraid to use his trusty Colt 45. Louis L'Amour was another author I devoured. He wrote smashing cowboy frontier stories that were always in high demand in the nicks I went in. Then I got into Jeffrey Archer, the MP and deputy chairman of the Conservative Party, who ended up doing a bit of time himself in the nick. *Kane and Abel* is a top read.

I was given a date for my release and was taken into Maidstone town centre to get kitted out. The civilian clothes I'd come in with ten or eleven years earlier would probably be sufficient to qualify for my immediate re-arrest. The idea was that the state would pay up to a certain amount for a suit, shirt, tie and shoes to give you half a chance should you get a job interview as you struggled to re-enter society. I spent all of my allowance on an upmarket pair of snazzy brown brogue shoes. Church's, of course. I'd already had my suit made to measure in the nick, where there was a workshop for tailoring.

When the screws came to unlock me and walk me down the stairs, my fellow prisoners came out the cells, applauded me and started to sing 'For He's a Jolly Good Fellow', which brought a lump to my throat. After all, we'd spent years – some of us – in close proximity, and were privy to each other's loves and hates, hopes and fears, highs and lows. Many friendships made in prison last until one or the other of you dies, and they run very deep. Even if you go years without reconnecting, when you do that intense shared experience ensures the bond soon comes to the surface.

A single officer took me outside and shook my hand. Another officer passed us by the gates and huffed, 'Very funny.' Me and my escort exchanged a puzzled look.

'I hope I never see you again, Ronnie.'

'I bet you say that to all the cons.'

We laughed and patted one another's backs.

Beyond the second officer in the road was Stan the Man, parked up in a gleaming Rolls-Royce, which certainly wouldn't have been his. Next to him in the passenger seat grinning like a Cheshire cat was Cornish Mick. Stan the Man was a local businessman whose preferred sailing course was close to the wind. He ran the fruit and veg stall outside the Red Lion pub, spent money as quickly as he acquired it and was a Del Boy character before John Sullivan invented him. I got in the back. A bottle of vodka, a bottle of tonic and a bucket of ice was kindly set up for me.

'You upset that screw?' I asked.

'He tried to move us on,' explained Stan. 'I told him I was here to pick up the governor. You're the Guvnor.'

We all laughed, and Stan revved up, waved to the screws and we sped off to freedom.

11

FREEDOM COME, FREEDOM GO

The old firm had broken up after ten years out of action. Although the others should all have been out well before me on account of their lesser sentences, Pat was still inside. He'd escaped from Maidstone jail, only to be recaptured by the army and getting an extra three years for his trouble. He ended up back in Parkhurst, and when he was eventually released we commandeered a Roller and went and picked him up. I saw Colin only a couple of times after my release, but I got the distinct impression he was uncomfortable to see me. I think I reminded him of a part of his life he preferred to forget and had put behind him, and I guess he was dreading me asking him, 'Want a bit of work?' I understood that.

Terry also had no intention of risking more bird. That surprised me, as he was an enthusiastic, daring and bloody good armed robber, and he'd joined me on so many other bits of work too. Terry bought himself a fish and chip shop in Cambridgeshire and led a quieter life. Frying instead of firing. Who can blame him? Bursting into banks brandishing shotguns isn't for everyone. Especially as you get older. Terry was one of those people in my life whose friendship I'll always treasure. He was a good man and a good mate.

Joe welcomed me back to the fold and very generously gave me a 'drink' of many thousands of pounds that he'd collected from our friends and associates, adding a healthy topping-up from his own funds. I was grateful for such a generous gesture. It was enough to buy a small gaff if I'd fancied it and a new car for the drive. I bought a number of posh motors – a Roller for a very brief period – but unsurprisingly these attracted the attention of the police, and I couldn't get out of Sutton without a tug. I had to tone it down. There were some different people around Joe now, and I had to make new friends and associates. One of them, Del, became one of Joe's most loyal companions, and has remained a good and true friend and reliable ally of mine to this day.

There were practical everyday problems to overcome too. Sadie asked me to drive her to McDonald's. I thought McDonald was an old codger who had a farm, but apparently it was a new fast-food burger chain from America fast putting the old familiar Wimpy Bars out of business. I drove the car up Throwley Way in Sutton.

'Dad!' screamed Sadie. 'What are you doing?!'

I wondered why the cars were coming towards me all across the road and sounding their horns. They'd installed a whole new one-way system in Sutton in my absence. How remiss of the council not to write to me in Parkhurst and let me know about their plans.

Besides alcohol having become more expensive, I also noticed that people as well as the roads had changed in the last decade. Everyone seemed to have speeded up. To me it was very noticeable. Before you'd see housewives putting down their shopping, pulling their groceries behind them in trolleys and stopping to chat to each other. Now most of them were in cars, driving into multi-storey car parks and filling their boots from a wire trolley. Barely a word was exchanged.

Young people were calling themselves 'yuppies', running around from meeting to meeting clutching ridiculous overflowing Filofaxes, overdosing on self-importance. They spent most of the time telling each other how busy they were, promising a 'window' next Thursday at 2.07 p.m. Spare time was sneered at. Having little or nothing to do was a shame not to be admitted.

I was surprised to come across video recorders. It took a while for my brain to process the concept of being able to tape moving images and sound from the television. Chunky cassette tapes were now piled up next to tellies in most homes and pirated new Hollywood films were being premiered in the nation's sitting rooms before the cinemas. The world was moving fast and speeding up.

On a personal level, I didn't have anywhere to live. Carol's mum Thelma had some friends, Joan and Alan, and they very charitably allowed me to stay with them. They were straight-goers and in no way connected to the criminal world. Then I moved in with Carol and Sadie in a short-lived reconciliation.

Not long after I was out, Joey Pyle took me to meet Charlie Kray. We met in a wine bar. Wine bars had suddenly become all the rage. They were just pubs, really, now rebranded, although women felt more comfortable in them than they did in the noisy and raucous public bars of pubs. Bottles of Blue Nun and Black Tower white wine were being shifted by the box load, gold Benson & Hedges cigarette packets lay open on most tables and ashtrays overflowed.

Charlie was standing there tall, dressed impeccably in a pin-stripe suit with a silk white handkerchief strategically placed in the breast pocket. Beneath he wore a quality white shirt, probably from Jermyn Street. A handsome man with slightly long hair for his age, he had a broad, welcoming smile and softer features than his twin brothers. He was with one of his co-defendants from the 1969 trial, Tony Lambriano, a nice man too. Charlie, Tony and Joe all embraced once we'd threaded through the crowd that surrounded them. Women as well as men clamoured for a slither of attention from a Kray brother.

By this time the Kray legend had grown tremendously with the publication of the book *The Profession of Violence*, which sold hundreds of thousands of copies and kickstarted a whole new genre of crime books. Everybody wanted a piece of the twins, but as they were incarcerated, Charlie was the best they could get. He was not complaining, though. Drinks and cigarettes were offered and enthusiastically accepted everywhere, and our table practically tipped over with Charlie's favourite tipple of Scotch and Coke with ice. He was charming to me, as he was to everyone, and we hit it off straight away.

Later we visited the Blue Orchid and Scarlett's clubs in Croydon together, as well as other drinking gaffs. Wherever we went, people looked over cautiously at first – Charlie was a Kray, after all, and Joe also had a big reputation, but when they could see how amiable they both were, they came to say a few words. In those days before selfies, Charlie would happily sign autographs. When *The Krays* film came out starring the Kemp brothers from the band Spandau Ballet, the obsession with all things Kray went stratospheric. Barely a day would pass without one of the family being in the newspapers.

We spent a lot of time in a fantastic wine bar called Winners in Raynes Park. There was a smashing bunch of people in there for some years. Anyone who was anyone in the criminal world paid a visit at some time or other, and plenty of faces from entertainment and the sports world too. Actors from *EastEnders* and *The Bill*, who filmed their location stuff on an estate nearby, were often in, as were numerous boxers. One day the guvnor, Eddie, said to me that he thought we were going to lean on him for protection money. I laughed. He then said that bringing all the criminal and showbiz faces down that we did had done wonders for his takings. Perhaps we should have put our hand in your pocket, I joked.

I'll never forget the day the real Old Bill stormed in through the front and back doors brandishing guns.

'Everyone on the floor,' they screamed.

Bar a couple of interlopers, nobody moved. We just looked over at them with mild amusement. They were looking for an armed robber – a good young friend of mine – who'd made a daring escape from a prison van on the way to court and had managed to handcuff three security guards to some railings. It had been all over the papers. After the police were satisfied their quarry wasn't present, one of the detectives came over to me.

'You're fucking mad, you lot, you are. You could have had your brains blown out,' he said.

'Guns don't really faze us,' I replied.

'Anywhere else where armed police storm in they'd still have been on the floor now.'

'Would you like a drink?' I asked.

I was in Winners one night when a bloke turned up who'd been close to Reggie Kray in prison and was his gofer. Now he was out on home leave. Reggie was apparently very fond of him, and didn't this chap let you know it. He believed that his connection to Reg bestowed special status on him.

'Reg says you've got to give me an ounce of puff,' he demanded of me.

'Reg didn't say that.'

'He did.'

'Well, I'm not giving you an ounce of puff. I'm not even going to buy you a drink.'

'Reg will hear about this.'

'Yes, he will. From me. Before you even get back to the nick. Now fuck off.'

Unfortunately, the twins attracted all sorts of hangers-on, sycophants and parasites, and regrettably they couldn't always tell them apart from genuine people.

Winners used to attract a lot of office girls, and they'd often spend time in our company. They knew we were villains but didn't know exactly what we did. I don't think they cared. One girl was very naïve. She worked in a local building society and was married to the branch manager. One evening she excused herself, saying she had to be home early because there was a 'big delivery' coming in the morning and her husband had to be there. A big delivery? Well, what could a building society be having a big delivery of? Not sand or cement. Could only be cash.

Me and an accomplice were there the next morning, masked up and armed. When we demanded the bags that had just been deposited, the manager panicked and pulled one of the cashier girls in front of him like a shield. I was shocked and disgusted, and felt like shooting him. Realising how cowardly his action was, he stepped from behind his staff member and handed over the bags.

The following week the girl was in the wine bar recounting the story of the raid. When she described the bravery of her husband, remaining calm and only handing over some of the bags, apparently, I wanted to tell her the truth.

'Your husband sounds like a brave man,' I said instead.

'It takes a lot to scare my Dennis,' she replied.

There was a bloke who came in Winners a lot who looked like me. Others pointed it out, and I could see the likeness. He got off on being around us and I noticed he started dressing like me. Turning up in suits and all that caper. I used to call him over to join our group. He was pleased as punch and flattered. What he didn't know was I'd called him into my close proximity because I figured if somebody came in to shoot me they might take him out instead.

I visited Ron Kray regularly in Broadmoor around this time, at his invitation. Normally Joe Pyle and I would drive there. Approaching Broadmoor for the first time is a sombre experience. The red-bricked Victorian entrance with its two towers and arched entrance had the look of a church crossed with a concentration camp. Ron had no restrictions on visitors, as far as I could make out. When we arrived, normally somebody was leaving, and when we left, someone else had already rolled up and was waiting. Ron would enter dressed as if he was attending a wedding. The residents were patients, not prisoners, and allowed to wear their own clothes. He'd be immaculately attired wearing a Savile Row tailored suit, smart tie and pressed Persil-white shirt, with black shoes so shiny you could adjust your tie by them. Ron had been known to leave a meeting in disgust or dismiss a visitor if they didn't come suitably attired themselves or were late.

'If I can make the time, why can't they?' Ron complained to me once.

'You've got a lot of time, though, Ron.'

I wanted to slurp the words back in as they came out, but it was too late. I'd blurted something out I shouldn't have done. I thought, *What have I fucking done?* Ron peered at me over his glasses, a hint of displeasure in the look, but said nothing. I think I blotted my copy book there.

The visits normally followed a routine.

'Would you like anything from the canteen, Ron?' Joe or I would ask politely when a member of staff came around taking orders.

'That's very kind of you, Ronnie. Do you mind getting me two hundred cigarettes, please?'

I had a coffee and slice of Victoria sponge in mind.

'No problem, Ron.'

'That's very kind of you, Ronnie. I know it's a bit of a liberty, but would you mind getting two hundred for my friend Jonathan. I do like to look after others if I can in here.'

I've no idea if there was a Jonathan or not in Broadmoor. But whoever they were for, they sure smoked a lot of fags. I'm certain we weren't the only visitors Ron was making the same request to.

One afternoon we broke for lunch, and Joe and I went to a pub in the village nearby. As we were eating at our table, I spotted a lady holding a tray and looking over at us, smiling. I recognised her from the television and newspapers as Sonia Sutcliffe, wife of Peter, the Yorkshire Ripper.

'Sonia Sutcliffe's coming over,' I whispered to Joe.

'Tell her to fuck off,' hissed Joe out the side of his mouth.

But Sonia was placing her tray down on our table.

'Mind if I join you,' she asked nicely.

Joe glared at her. 'Yes, we do.'

A hurt-looking Sonia walked away and found another table.

'What's she doing even visiting that misfit?' Joe said.

Another time Ron announced, 'Ronnie, please take this.' He passed me a folded piece of paper torn from a lined exercise book. 'Please don't look at it until you're off the premises. Thank you.'

Back in the car I took the note from my breast pocket. It was a list of about a dozen names and nothing else. I recognised most as villains; others were journalists, and the legal profession was represented. There was even one showbusiness personality.

'What's this all about, Joe?'

Joe was laughing.

'He wants you to kill them.'

'What!'

'Yes, he told me when you were in the toilet.'

'Is he mad?'

'Well, he is in Broadmoor.'

'I can't do that. Twelve! That's ridiculous.'

'Just ignore it. Throw it away. He'll have forgotten by the next time we come.'

'Why is he asking me?'

'Well, I said to Ron, anything you want done, just ask Ronnie.'

'Thanks, Joe.'

'I said, "Anything you want done" not "Anyone".'

It was fine for Joe – he wasn't the one who had been given the task to execute. I was agitated the next time we visited.

'How many off that list have you done?' asked Joe, laughing, as we approached the gate.

'Fuck off, Joe. It's not funny.'

As we stood waiting in the reception area a known face came out. He was one of the twins' East End friends. We exchanged pleasantries.

'Ron's in good form,' he remarked.

I couldn't reply because I was temporarily speechless.

'What's up, Ronnie?' asked Joe.

'That geezer is top of Ron's list!'

We could do nothing but laugh. Inside Ronnie was sitting erect, and when we came in he stood up and shook our hands enthusiastically.

'You know that list,' said Ron almost immediately, even before ordering industrial quantities of cigarettes.

'Yes,' I replied hesitantly, thinking, *Here we go.*

'You haven't done any, have you? I haven't read anything or seen any reports on the telly.'

'No, Ron.'

'Good, destroy it, please.'

Thank God, I thought. *He's seen sense.*

'I've got a new one.'

My heart sank as he passed over another piece of carefully folded paper. When I looked at it later there were about ten completely different names. One name was crossed out and then added again at the bottom. God only knows what this poor chap had done to upset Ron. He gave me four or five of these lists in total. I knew the lists were the work of Ron and Ron alone because there were a couple of names of people that were close to Reg on there. If they'd been taken out, I don't think he'd have been best pleased.

I was half expecting to find my own name on one of the lists when I hadn't carried out his wishes. I'd see people in clubs, pubs and charity events boasting about how close they were to Ron and Reg, and think to myself, 'Yes, mate, but do you realise you were on hit list three, number seven?' I'd see a certain television personality and laugh inside that he had absolutely no knowledge that a Kray twin had murderous intent towards him.

Ron got married about this time – his second wife – to a confident, lovely lady called Kate Howard. Ron asked Joe if he'd supply a bodyguard for the now Kate Kray as she'd become a high-profile name in her own right. Joe said, 'Ronnie will do it', and I did for a couple of years. Kate and I got on great, and we remain good friends to this day. What I particularly liked was that Kate didn't drink, and this meant that when we went to the numerous parties, book signings and personal appearances, I could have a bit of booze as Kate wouldn't mind driving home. I attended their wedding reception, which was a good bash, even though the groom and Reg could not be there. Later they divorced, and Kate forged a career as a bestselling author and television documentary maker.

In 1990 *The Krays* film I mentioned earlier was released. I never spoke to Reg about it, but Ron liked it on one visit and then didn't on the next. What he did get upset about was that Charlie – he alleged – had sold the video rights well under market value, or this is what he'd been told. The film turned out to be one of the bestselling British films ever on video, and later on DVD. At one point Ron's anger with Charlie was such that I even thought I might find his name on one of the hit lists that Ron kept popping in my breast pocket. On one visit to Ron, Joe and I went with Charlie, and he was clearly very edgy. Joe nudged me and nodded at Charlie's hand, which was visibly trembling as he tried to pull a cigarette out the packet. That was sad. Poor old Charlie got the blame for everything, even for things the twins mucked up. Although he was a loved brother, he was never treated equally by them.

I was grateful to Charlie because he got me in the film right at the end. You must be quick to see it but in the final scene at Violet Kray's funeral there are pairs of mourners spaced out and watching around Chingford Cemetery. I am there, standing with Joey Pyle, after the camera has panned onto Charlie. No further film offers were forthcoming.

The last time I saw Ron was in Broadmoor. Joe was there. Ron fixed his eyes on me. 'Your name's Ron, isn't it?'

Strange question to ask after twenty years.

'Yes, Ron, it is.'

He fiddled with his wrist and handed over to me a gold bracelet that was tucked under his cufflinked sleeves. The letters R O N were engraved on it. I paused. I didn't know if this was some sort of test. If I took it, would he think I was a shallow bastard on the take? If I refused, would he take offence?

'Take it. It's a gift.'

I took it and thanked him.

'Are you sure?'

He lifted an eyebrow, as if to say, *Don't ask silly questions*. I still have the bracelet today. For all the would-be burglars out there – I don't keep it at home. Later, Ronnie's wife Kate gifted me Ron's monogrammed cufflinks as a present to mark my daughter's wedding. I don't keep them at home either.

I'd gone out on my first blag a week after my release. I was thrilled to be back at work. I teamed up with a mate I'd made in Parkhurst – Blackie Saxton. Blackie, who was white-skinned, by the way, was a prolific criminal who was sentenced to more years in prison than he had on the planet. His record is worth a look. He was born in Nottingham in 1933 and had his first conviction before I was born. In 1950 he escaped from Rochester Borstal, and the following year he alarmed the press when he had it on his toes from Hull Borstal. In 1954, during his national service, he was in the headlines again when he and another soldier tunnelled out of a military prison in Yeovil.

Three years later he got his first lump of adult porridge for safe-blowing. On his release in 1960 he and some other men carried out an armed payroll robbery, stealing £11,000, worth £1 million at today's values. In 1962 he dramatically jumped from a train that was taking him from London to

Dartmoor Prison. He told me that he was in one of the old single carriages with the pull-down windows, and he ran and dived out of it. Luckily, a train wasn't coming the other way. Unluckily, he was recaptured an hour later. Ten years on he got another twelve stretch for armed robbery, and had three years added to his sentence for escaping from Leicester jail. In 1981 he was sent down again for a wages snatch at Addenbrooke's Hospital in Cambridge. He couldn't have been out long when he copped another seven for committing robberies while disguised as a policeman.

In 1988 the tabloid newspapers ran a story on how his long-lost daughter had hired a private detective who traced him to prison, and Blackie pledged to give up his life of crime so the reunited father and daughter could enjoy precious time together. The private detective was so touched that he waived his fee. However, Blackie was released soon after that article was published and he came to find me. In 1991, at the age of nearly sixty, he was sentenced to ten years in France for smuggling drugs. But in the period Blackie and I were at it we were very active and having it off. He was a fearless man and a staunch partner-in-crime.

He told me that he was on a job once when one of the lady customers he was watching over while his colleague went to work complained of feeling ill. He pulled up a chair for her and invited her to sit down.

'Thank you so much,' she said.

Having drawn out compassion in Blackie, she then asked, 'Would you mind if I took the chair and sat outside?'

'I don't think so, madam,' he replied.

I lost touch with Blackie, and a few years back now I was told he'd been murdered. Very sad. He was a good man.

Johnny Forder was another well-known armed robber I befriended in Parkhurst jail who came and found me in the early 90s. Johnny was coming to the end of a fourteen-year stretch when I met him. I remember him telling me he was banged up with the Hollywood actor Stacy Keach in Reading jail for a short time. Keach was famous for playing my favourite fictional detective Mike Hammer on screen and fell foul of our authorities for allegedly importing cocaine through Heathrow Airport, copping six months. Johnny had a tussle with the governor at Maidstone when they refused to allow him to keep some top-shelf magazines Stacy had sent in to him.

We got to drinking together with another friend of Johnny's, Terry Russell, who came out of Thamesmead. His nickname was Gumbo. Terry was a good money-getter, and was known to have a shrewd head on his shoulders. I'd be happy to be on a job with him. Our conversations soon turned to work, and Johnny and Terry invited me onto a job they had coming up. It sounded too good to be true. The boys had a man on the inside at Gatwick Airport who'd told them about a £10m consignment of diamonds that was being flown into the airport and then being taken on to its onward destination by private car so as not to arouse interest. Well, it aroused my interest. It could be my biggest blag yet.

'Ten million pounds' worth of diamonds. That's a lot of fucking diamonds. A lot of fucking money. Who are they for?' I asked.

'Us,' smiled Johnny.

Can't argue with that.

The only problem was that our man on the inside – let's call him Tom – couldn't say when the diamonds were coming. The schedule was being kept vague for security purposes. Tom knew they would be coming one morning following an overnight flight 'any day'. So we hid our guns near the airport, placed a couple of getaway cars at strategic points and met at the Gatwick Penta Hotel each morning. We'd have breakfast, five of us, splitting into two tables so as not to look too conspicuous waiting for the word. It didn't come. There was three or four days of this, and I was getting increasingly uncomfortable.

'I'm pulling off the job, Johnny,' I announced.

'Don't be daft. It's going to be on at any time,' he tried to reassure me.

'We'll qualify for a free breakfast and win hotel customer of the year at this rate. Something's not right. I'm pulling off, Johnny.'

Johnny and the others reluctantly accepted my decision. Then Johnny pleaded with me to drive him down the next day, and any further days after, and leave my gun for them to use.

'No, Johnny, I told you, I'm out. It's too suss.'

'We'll give you a hundred grand if we have it off.'

'What time do you want picking up?'

The very next day was the same again, but as we left the hotel and got into our cars to get on with our day all hell was let loose. Police cars came screeching in every entrance, skidding to an emergency stop. I wouldn't have been surprised to see Jack Regan leap out, followed by George Carter. Armed police stood up on the roof and balconies of the hotel, fixing their guns on us. More would-be shooters peered round corners, gripping their guns with two hands. Four *Sweeney*-type rozzers jumped out their motors and surrounded us, with their revolvers pointing at me in the driver's seat. Members of the public and hotel staff were ignoring roars of 'Keep clear!' and 'Go inside!' to watch the spectacle from a distance. We all had our hands held up very, very high.

'Wind the fucking window down!' demanded the lead copper.

'You wind the fucking window down,' I yelled back.

I knew that had I lowered my hands to open the window, this highly charged Old Bill with bulging eyes and a twitchy finger in front of me would have pumped bullets into my chest. That's what he wanted. And if he was really bent, he would have dropped a spare gun from his pocket into my lap and even wrapped my hand around it.

As he threw open my door, I shouted at the top of my voice so the bystanders could clearly hear, 'I'm unarmed! I'm unarmed!'

The police dragged me out the seat with me still shouting that I was unarmed, and they put a foot on my neck, yanked my hands behind my back and cuffed me up. Then they lifted me into the back of a plain-clothes police car and tore off to Crawley nick.

Two detectives sat either side of me, and there were two more in the front. They all seemed very wound up. Back at the station one copper came up to me, stood close and said very quietly, 'You know you and Forder were supposed to go, don't you?'

'What do you mean?'

'You know what I fucking mean.'

12

WE'RE THE SWEENEY, SON

Because me and Johnny hadn't been killed or permanently disabled, I believe they were looking on what I later found out they called Operation Angel as a part failure. It's my belief that the Sweeney at the time were operating a shoot-to-kill policy. 'The Sweeney' was of course rhyming slang for the Flying Squad – Sweeney Todd, Flying Squad – although I don't remember too many people referring to the Sweeney in everyday conversation until the television series *The Sweeney* burst into our living rooms in the mid-1970s. 'The Filth' was more common.

The Flying Squad first came into existence within the Metropolitan Police as the Mobile Patrol Experiment in 1919, with a brief to perform surveillance and collect intelligence on criminals, especially thieves, using a horse-drawn carriage with peepholes cut into the sides. The architect of this first incarnation of the squad was a detective called Fred Wensley, who'd been an original beat copper on the Jack the Ripper murders investigation that started in 1888.

Soon the Mobile Patrol Experiment was deemed a success and made permanent, changing its name to the Flying Squad (and later the Central Robbery Squad), reflecting the ability of its detectives to range across London without being hampered by divisional policing boundaries and red tape. By the 1950s the squad was known for flying around the capital in fast cars, bells ringing, intercepting armed robberies.

The Sweeney television series first aired in 1975 and ran to 1978, but it's replayed to this day. It took the viewing public by storm. Never before had a television police programme presented such a gritty, nuanced and realistic view of the never-ending battle between police and criminals. Sergeant Dixon of *Dixon of Dock Green* was more likely to offer you a Werther's Original than the swift knee in the bollocks Jack Regan could deliver. Later *Z Cars* and *Softly, Softly* went a little way down the road of showing some police as flawed characters, but stopped short of tackling police brutality and corruption.

The Sweeney, spearheaded by John Thaw as Inspector Jack Regan and Dennis Waterman as his sidekick, loyal Detective Sergeant George Carter, was smack bang in your face. The pair were boozers, shaggers, scrappers and proud thief-takers, and they'd never let a bit of protocol get in the way of a good nicking. If a blagger had to be set up for the perceived public good, so be it. They were quick to snatch their guns from their shoulder holsters and take people out. The programme demonstrated that not all police were all good and not all robbers were all bad. It trod the thin line between effective police and effective criminals. As an armed robber I loved it. Never before and never since has a television programme got so close to the real thing and captured an era and a criminal group so accurately. When we got televisions in prison and it was repeated, it was a big favourite.

The Sweeney's – and specialist police firearms units' – shoot-to-kill policy isn't just fantasy on my part. Just a few years before the Gatwick ambush, a seasoned robber and good man named Ronnie Easterbrook and his pal Tony Ashe were pounced upon in similar circumstances by the Flying Squad as they swapped cars after raiding a Bejam store in Woolwich. The police shot Tony twice – in the neck and chest – and killed him, and arrested Ronnie, but not before he'd put a bullet in one of them. The police hated Ronnie, and he them. He'd been around a long time, having first appeared in court in 1949.

Ronnie was imprisoned for life after the judge said he 'represented a threat to all law-abiding citizens'. He later confided in me in prison that he hadn't even wanted to go on that bit of work. The haul was expected to only be £12,000, which was not really worth the risk to him. But Tony Ashe was his pal, and was down on his luck financially and personally, so Ronnie only went along as a favour.

Just before his sentencing, Ronnie had made a dramatic escape bid when he smuggled explosives into a high-security prison van and blew a hole in its side. I heard that the explosives were smuggled into the prison inside packets of caviar.

Unluckily, all the debris fell on Ronnie, and he was trapped beneath and unable to complete his escape.

After sentencing at the Old Bailey, Ronnie declared that he hated all police officers and that he'd wanted to die in that armed exchange. He added that he was convinced that police planned that day to assassinate him and Tony. He told me he only shot the policeman because the copper was going to shoot him as he lay on the ground. The Flying Squad denied there was a shoot-to-kill policy. Thirty years earlier Ronnie had been sentenced to ten years for shooting another policeman, and the police never forget.

Ronnie sent a wreath to Tony's funeral with a photograph pinned to it of the man he believed had tipped police off about the Bejam raid. One day when we were at the Belmarsh Unit together, we returned from exercise and went to Ronnie's cell, where an official-looking letter was lying on his bed. He opened it and then tossed it contemptuously to one side.

'Bad news, Ronnie?' I asked.

'Usual shit. They changed me to a natural life sentence.'

And that's what happened, despite hunger strikes, legal actions and appeals to the European Court of Human Rights, where they'd ruled that the tariff-fixing procedure had been unlawful. Ronnie died in 2009 in Gartree Prison, aged seventy-seven and defiant to the end. In the armed robbery community, Ronnie Easterbrook is a legend.

In 1983 the police shot and nearly killed the completely innocent man Stephen Waldorf when they mistook him for

David Martin, a dangerous criminal they had under surveillance. It's OK, though, because when Waldorf was recovering in hospital from being shot multiple times and pistol-whipped, Scotland Yard visited him and apologised.

Only two years before the Gatwick job, well-known armed robber Kenny Baker was shot dead by Met Police marksmen during an attempted raid on a Securicor van in Reigate, Surrey. Mehmet Arif, who was driving that day, has always said there was no warning from police. Kenny was shot in the torso and face. The papers reported he was wearing a Ronald Reagan mask. This sad day was very much in my mind when the police closed in on the car that morning at the Penta Hotel.

It emerged that my misgivings about the Gatwick job were well founded. Our firm were under obbo before I was even recruited to the job. There was a grass somewhere along the line, the police having been tipped off about the planned robbery some time back. They'd been watching Johnny and Terry's every move, they'd seen the cars and where we were stashing the guns, and were all over the hotel with us each morning. Who knows, they could have been at the next table passing me the tomato sauce. I don't think for one minute the leak came from any of us five. But someone somewhere had overheard something. Loose lips and all that. I don't know who and don't want to know.

I met Tom again years later and he seemed nervous.

'Are you OK, Tom?' I asked.

'Yes,' he replied sheepishly.

'Come on, what's the matter?'

'Well, the police told me that when you came out you'd most probably kill me.'

I laughed.

'Were they trying to get you to tell them something at the time?'

'Yes, they were.'

'There you go, Tom.'

He seemed relieved.

We had to wait a whole year to go to trial, and I spent my first remand day in Lewes jail, a new one for me. Lewes very quickly said they didn't want us and told our guards to take us away.

'We don't take Cat A's here,' the jail explained.

'I'm Cat B,' I protested.

'Not anymore you're not,' and we were whisked off to Brixton.

I'd barely been at liberty for three years. When I was in Brixton Prison I was officially made a Double A Cat prisoner for the first time. It was while on remand in Brixton that two IRA men made a dramatic escape. Nessan Quinlivan and Pearse McAuley were awaiting trial for conspiracy to murder Sir Charles Tidbury, chairman of Whitbread, the giant brewing company. He was considered a legitimate target by the IRA because he was a fundraiser for events commemorating the 300th anniversary of the 'Glorious Revolution' of 1688.

The two men, who were also both Cat A prisoners, were returning from chapel when one produced a small pistol that had been smuggled into the jail in a hollowed-out section of a shoe. I heard that a nun brought the gun in for them, but that could just have been a rumour. They took a warden hostage, holding the gun to his head, and made their way out of the prison buildings and over the wall, discharging the pistol a couple of times. Outside they hijacked a car, shooting a man in the leg in the process, and then hailed a black cab, which dropped them at Baker Street tube station. Good job Uber weren't around as the driver would probably have got lost.

Us other Cat As had no idea of their plans – I didn't know the men, as I'd only just arrived – but their ingenuity and audacity were breathtaking. There was uproar and heads rolled. The governor of the prison was nudged into early retirement, some other civil servants lost their jobs, and the Home Secretary – another Kenny Baker – only held on to his position by the skin of his teeth.

Shortly after the breakout a heavily escorted bunch of men in suits arrived. They were carrying out some sort of enquiry and I leant over the balcony to look down on them. The con next to me said one of the bigwigs was Lord Woolf, but I wouldn't have known him if he'd pissed on my shoes. Then I noticed another of the visitors looking up at me and smiling. It was Tony, whose garden I'd tended a few years back. He was obviously now something important at the Home Office. He gestured as if to say 'Stay there' – I don't know where he thought I could go. He came up the stairs, shook my hand warmly and motioned for me to walk back into my cell.

I did as he asked, but when he started to close the cell door behind him I said, 'Leave it open, Guv. I don't want anyone saying I'm a grass or anything, do I?'

'Sorry, Ronnie, of course. What was I thinking?'

He said he recognised me straight away. What was I doing here? Was everything OK? How did I find Brixton? He didn't ask me about the escape; he knew I wouldn't say anything anyway. The very next day I was moved to a new experimental Double A Cat unit at Belmarsh Prison, of which more in the next chapter.

The Gatwick trial at Croydon Crown Court was held amid 'the tightest security operation ever known there', according to the *Croydon Advertiser*, and it lasted more than two months. Armed police were in and around the court every day. Most of us were charged with conspiracy to commit armed robbery, to which we pleaded not guilty, but the jury couldn't decide, so the judge dismissed them and brought in a lesser charge of conspiracy to steal, to which we pleaded guilty. I got three and a half years, and they took me down.

I served the next three years in various prisons, some familiar to me and some not. While I was away Joey Pyle came in, having been set up by undercover police over a drugs deal. It was his first sentence since the Cooney case back in 1960. I was both pleased and not pleased to see him, if you know what I mean. His thirty-year-plus run at the top of the tree had been unprecedented and it was sad for me to see him in the nick. He didn't belong there. Joe always seemed untouchable to me, royalty in our circles. There were some lessons to be learned about Joe's 1992 case around undercover operations that I should have taken on board but didn't.

Although Joe was the guvnor in prison, he was one of the boys too. He didn't throw his weight around and just got on with his bird. He wouldn't have it with the screws, though. If they spoke to him he'd be civil and reply, but he wasn't one for conversing with them. Truth is, they feared him. They knew that Joe may have been inside but his power on the outside was undiminished, and they wouldn't risk upsetting him. When he later went to Coldingley Prison in Surrey, they had to put him down for doing some type of work.

'What do you know about computers, Joe?'

'Nothing. Never switched one on.'

'Good, we'll put you down for computers.'

'Told you I don't know anything about them.'

'Don't worry, Joe, we haven't got any computers.'

My good friend Kevin picked me up on release this time and very generously took me to live with him initially, as again I'd nowhere to go. He also very kindly bought me a car. In 1995 I'd not been out long when Ron Kray died. His funeral was a sad day and a momentous occasion. The comparison has been made before, but I can't think of another funeral up to that time since Winston Churchill's in 1965 that brought the people out in such numbers. Our great prime minister and wartime leader's funeral was a state occasion. Ronnie's was an estate one. It was one of the final large-scale public show-outs by those salt-of-the-earth working-class London people who fought and endured the Second World War, and lived mainly in council flats and houses on estates across the capital.

I travelled to Ron's funeral in Roy Shaw's Rolls-Royce. We knew it was going to be a big affair, but the closer we got to St Matthew's Church in Bethnal Green, the deeper the crowds lining both sides of the road became, many of them from the 'wrong side of the streets'. Outside the undertakers the chaps gathered, men in Crombie overcoats merging into one great cashmere blob. If you looked closely, broken noses, chewed ears and scars galore were everywhere. Behind crash barriers the people stood patiently, waiting for a glimpse of Ron's coffin and the arrival of Reg himself from Maidstone Prison. When he appeared, the huge crowd gasped as one and broke into applause. When I saw Reg's floral tribute on the hearse it bought a lump to my throat – TO THE OTHER HALF OF ME.

A couple of us walked down to the church, and as we approached the door a bald, youngish bloke who seemed to be in charge held up his hand. He had a cheeky grin, laced with a shot of menace.

'Sorry, my friend, you can't go in there. Invitation only. Besides, it's packed.'

Who is this fucking geezer? I thought.

'Is Charlie Kray inside?'

'Yes, he is.'

'Can you tell him Ronnie Field's outside?'

'Ronnie. Sorry. Follow me.'

The bloke I learned was Dave Courtney, and Reg had hired him to manage the security for the day. He had a doorman, bouncer and bodyguard army at his beck and call, and it was generally agreed he did a good job. Little did he know, and I know, that we'd soon be spending a lot of time together in closer proximity. After the church we travelled behind scores of limos to Chingford Cemetery for the burial, and then we ended the day at Charlie Breaker's pub, I think. These days I get my funerals mixed up; I've been to so many.

We had a mate with us that day – let's call him Donald. Me and Joe liked him until one day I got a phone call from his son saying that he'd been interfering with his children, Donald's own grandchildren. The following morning I was having breakfast at Joe's when the doorbell rang. I answered it.

'Who is it?' shouts Joe.

'Donald,' I said. I'd already told him he wasn't coming in. Joe came to the door.

'You don't know how lucky you are,' Joe said. 'If it wasn't for that camera across the road you'd be a dead man.'

The police had long installed a spy camera to monitor the comings and goings at Joe's house. Donald left. I believe he was taken to court, but the case collapsed because the children's parents didn't want to put them through the trauma of giving evidence. It goes to show how we can all get people wrong.

The camera I mentioned was in the bedroom of the house opposite, and from time to time we'd give it a wave. Normally we'd sit in the kitchen of Joe's house, unless the racing was on the television in the lounge. Joe had an interest in some betting shops but also loved a punt. Not the best of combinations. A regular stream of visitors from the boxing and film worlds bearing gifts in the form of bottles of Jameson's would drop in and out. If we didn't meet there before Joe became ill, we'd still frequent the Red Lion in Sutton and the Crown in Morden.

Once Joe's wife got a call from a man who lived further down the same road. He said he thought Joe should speak to his lawyer urgently.

'Why?' Shirley asked.

'Because at 4.30 this morning under the cover of darkness I saw a man putting something into the boot of Joe's car, and his body language suggested to me he was doing something he shouldn't have been.'

Sure enough Joe's car was raided, and a gun found in the boot. Joe knew nothing about the gun and would never have been so stupid to have a firearm at his home or in his car. It was a very poor set-up, typical of inadequate under-cover Old Bill, but Joe was remanded in custody on the strength of it.

In court the prosecution tried to discredit Joe's neighbour.

'I suggest you are only giving this evidence because you are an acquaintance and neighbour of Mr Pyle.'

'On the contrary,' he said. 'I detest the man and all he stands for, but what I saw being done was wrong.'

The case was chucked, and Joe was released from remand.

Out again, I soon reverted to armed robbery. Back on the pavement. I should have gone and done some straight work, but which employer was going to offer me a few grand a week and adrenaline rushes like nothing else? I had a partner who I could trust with my life – and often did – and we were prolific. We went out and got what we needed, and sometimes that meant two in a week. I can even remember doing two on one Friday, Friday being armed robbery day.

13

THE UNIT

I'd been the very first guest to arrive in the Belmarsh Unit until a couple of the Arif firm and the Gatwick boys turned up a few days later from Brixton jail. They were still sweeping up the wood chippings off the floor from doing the locks when they deposited me at Belmarsh. I spent time in the Unit during my second and third prison sentences, and, as they were close together, I cannot always remember what events occurred in which stay. So, I'll recall my Unit experiences as one in this chapter.

Remarkably, when it opened for business in 1991, Belmarsh Prison was the first adult prison to have been built in London since work finished on Wormwood Scrubs in 1891. Bearing in mind the growth in the capital's population in the following hundred years, that speaks volumes about the state's attitude towards investment in the penal system. The bulk of the prison is on a massive site near Thamesmead, south London, surrounded by a one-mile-long perimeter wall. Belmarsh has four house blocks, each made up of three

three-storey spurs. These spurs each contain forty-two single and double cells. The prison is connected by tunnel to Woolwich Crown Court, as I'd discover.

Within this prison lies another prison, the High Security Unit (HSU), where up to forty-eight of Britain's allegedly most dangerous prisoners are held. This is what has become known as the 'Belmarsh Unit' or 'The Unit.' The Unit was the only prison to hold Double A Category inmates in Britain, and it boasted that it was escape-proof. That's what they said at Colditz. So far, so good, though. Even though nobody has broken out, Ross Kemp of *EastEnders* fame managed to break in to film a television documentary. Grant, as I call him, spent a night in the prison for entertainment purposes; well, I spent the first days and nights ever in there – on my Jack Jones. It was a surreal experience, I can tell you. Like going to school and being the only pupil – and no teachers either.

To come out of each landing you had to move through air-locked doors and change clothes each time. The doors are locked and unlocked remotely, and I can only liken it to moving through a malign USS *Enterprise* on *Star Trek*. It was very oppressive; you had nothing, your every move scrutinised by CCTV cameras. Movement was discouraged and self-restricted, as passing from one part of the prison to another involved the constant removing and replacing of clothing, along with intrusive body searches.

At first, we were in our cells for twenty-three hours out of twenty-four. There were some German prisoners in with us for a very short time. I never knew what they were in for. Someone said they were from the Baader–Meinhof terrorist group but nobody, including the screws, seemed very sure. The German embassy people came in to see them and were so shocked at the conditions that they had them moved out in days.

Later we settled into a more civilised routine. The day started at eight o'clock. We were given twenty minutes for breakfast, then an hour of outdoor exercise, then an hour to use the gym and half an hour cleaning up the wing. The rest of the time that we spent out of our cells – five hours – was 'association' time. During this period, we could chat to one another, play pool or table football, watch television, or use the rowing machine or exercise bike. Association is good and necessary, but there wasn't much point in opening a conversation with 'Been up to much?'

Alleged misbehaviour was dealt with by punishment in the form of being banished to the Seg (segregation) unit, where you'd spend twenty-three hours a day in a cell. And if you became particularly troublesome you'd get put in 'The Box', a room with nothing inside it except a Perspex window. No toilet. Just a bucket.

Us twelve on our landing were supposed to be the dozen prisoners in the penal system who were most likely to escape, and if we did so would pose the greatest danger to society as we'd have the resources and abilities to remain at large. That's what they told me, at least. They also said they wanted us in here so we wouldn't be a bad influence on other prisoners. It was far too late to be a bad influence on each other. We became graded as Double A Category, but the official terminology was 'Category A High Risk'. At various points during my spells in the Unit I shared time with the likes of Ronnie Easterbrook, Joe Pyle, Charlie Kray, various Arif brothers, Dingus Magee and other IRA men, Big John and Tony, Johnny Forder, Terry Russell, Charlie Bronson, and who can forget Dave Courtney? After my time came the Islamic terrorists. At any given occasion many of the prisoners in the Unit are household names.

'We get a lot of high-profile prisoners, and prisoners who have the means and capacity to escape,' one of the prison managers explained to the press. 'The type of prisoner we have here is a lot different to the type of prisoner in the normal prison. The prisoners here have the means and ability to achieve the results prisoners somewhere else would not.'

When Dave Courtney arrived it was like a whirlwind had hit the Unit. Dave was a good decade younger than me, and I didn't know him on the outside, except when we met at Ron Kray's funeral. But his name came up more and more. He's been accused of claiming he was part of the Kray gang when simple maths tells you he was still in short trousers when the twins got lifed off. He never said that – he said that the Krays were close friends and trusted him, which they clearly were and did. Dave was remanded into the Unit while awaiting trial on drugs charges, but the authorities must have seen him as a serious player or they would never have him remanded into Belmarsh Unit.

Dave was a charismatic cheeky chappie and a tough man underneath, both physically and mentally. They told him that Belmarsh would break him, and he said, 'No, it fucking will not.' He played them at their own games, winding them up, annoying them and making more work for them. If anything, Dave would break the screws and the managers, not the other way around. He had a quick wit and a fast brain. He should have gone on stage. Actually, he did. After his acquittal, Dave built a successful straight career as a writer, film-maker, actor, host, master of ceremonies, podcaster, and anything that involved getting his smiling face in front of camera. He paved the way for many of Britain's old villains to make a straight living in their old age. I'm forever grateful to Dave for saving my life – more on that later – and making a year of my life in the Unit not only more bearable, but thoroughly entertaining.

I remember when Joe Pyle came in on remand for the drugs fit-up and was arguing his case that he was a legitimate businessman operating in the film and music industries, that his underworld days were behind him. It was not beyond the realms of possibility for that to be the case. George Walker, who used to work with top 1950s gangster Billy Hill, became the chief executive of Brent Walker, which owned the Brent Cross Shopping Centre and the William Hill (Billy Hill, again) betting shop chain, among many other things. Joe Pyle came in my cell one day and showed me a card he'd received. It was from John Gotti, boss of the Gambino family in New York City. Mr Gotti, or the 'Teflon Don' as he was often known on account of the difficulty the FBI had in making any charges against him stick, was sending Joe a message of support and encouragement. Naturally, this letter would have been read and passed by the prison authorities to the police.

'That's all I fucking need,' sighed Joe.

One day a warder who I didn't know too well came to my cell and unlocked it. This was after him having put a prisoner in a cell opposite me and leaving him unlocked. I didn't know who'd just arrived, but they must have been somebody important as they'd landed by helicopter. We all heard it whirring in the grounds, and I thought for a moment it might have been Joey Pyle coming to join us.

'Do you want a shower, Ronnie?'

It was an unusual offer out the blue, but a shower was a luxury, and I'd have had three a day if it had been permitted.

'Yes, please,' I replied.

The screw leaned forward and whispered in my ear.

'There's a child killer in there.'

I knew that was a lie and was confused as to what I was being set up for. But a shower is a shower.

'Really?'

No way. Nonces were never put in with us, and they certainly did not chauffeur them around in helicopters.

When I entered the shower block the new prisoner looked over at me and nodded.

'All right, mate,' he said in a thick Belfast accent.

I nodded back.

'What have they told you I am?'

'They said you're a child murderer.'

'I'm an IRA man.'

I'd guessed that. The accent.

'I don't really have it with bombers,' I said, trying to bring the conversation to a close.

'I'm no bomber,' replied the Irishman firmly. 'I'm a soldier. I shoot people.'

He could see I was still not warming to him.

'I take out legitimate targets in the armed struggle.'

He told me his history, and I told him a bit of mine. I think many of the IRA men had time for us because, as they said, 'after all you're fighting the Establishment, like we are'. And some of us had time for some of them on an individual basis. Their bottle, daring, commitment and dogged determination could not be denied. Even inside they obeyed the orders of their military superiors and behaved like prisoners of war, although you couldn't get away from the fact that they were at war with us and ours.

I later learned the man in the shower was Paul Magee, but I called him by his nickname 'Dingus'. He escaped during his trial in Belfast for shooting dead a policeman and the highest-ranking SAS soldier to be killed in Northern Ireland. Magee went on to shoot two policemen over here and one died, and he later escaped from Whitemoor jail. He'd eventually be a beneficiary of Tony Blair's Good Friday Agreement, where former IRA terrorists received amnesties from prosecution and punishment.

Many, many years later my brother Ted was on a fishing holiday in the Republic of Ireland, and he fell into conversation with another angler on the riverbank. Ted said he noticed a couple of times the Irishman by his side looking intently at him as the gentle conversation flowed like the river.

'Where you from, Ted?'

'Rose Hill.'

'That near Raynes Park and Sutton area?'

'Yes.'

'What's your surname?'

'Field.'

'Have you got a brother?'

'Three.'

'You look very familiar, Ted. I think I was on a long holiday with one of your brothers some years ago. Ronnie?'

'You got it.'

Small world.

That prison officer was a wrong'un. If I'd attacked and hurt the 'child killer' it would have seen me charged, with years added to my sentence. And an IRA man would have been done. The officer wins on both counts. If the Irishman had attacked and hurt me, he would have had years added to his and I could have been battered, or worse. See how they can play their wicked and potentially fatal games?

In case you're thinking that the tales of cruelty and brutality from the prison officers are exaggerated or even invented by myself and other prisoners with an axe to grind, I'm going to quote a passage from a book called *The Loose Screw*, published in 2002. It's written by a former prison officer by the name of Jim Dawkins. He became disillusioned with the institutional physical and mental violence and brutality he encountered daily in the prison system, and decided to blow the lid on it. I must be candid and admit I don't remember Jim, nor do I recognise his photograph in the book, but I do recall the incident he recounts. I would, because as you'll see, I nearly died.

We had a prisoner called Ronnie Fields [sic] on the Unit at the time, who to inmates was an icon and to the officers a pain in the arse. He didn't give a fuck and absolutely hated screws and wasn't shy of letting them know this. He was, however, a gentleman and, so long as you didn't try any of the usual mind tricks or attempt to fuck up his routine, he just got on with his bird with dignity. He was a great friend of Dave Courtney's, but once again was hated by the bad element of staff. He could, however, handle himself very well and had demonstrated this by knocking out a good few screws and cons in his time. So, although he was the centre of most ego-boosting conversations in the officers' tearoom, no one would ever have had the bottle to take him out in the way they did other less hardy prisoners.

One afternoon the Irish lads decided to stage one of their regular weekend protests, which usually culminated in the spur getting flooded with a dozen or so officers from the 'elite' security department, who would use heavy-handed tactics to get all the inmates secured back in their cells. Whilst this was going on it became apparent that Ronnie had collapsed on the floor and was clearly having trouble breathing. Dave went to his aid immediately and sat on the floor with him in his arms, trying to help him control his breathing. Shortly afterwards the remainder of the spur had been secured and the alarm had been raised, but Ronnie was suffering a heart attack and was in a pretty bad way. Due to the security procedures involved in getting an ambulance into the unit, it usually took a minimum of half an hour for the paramedics to arrive.

What happened next will surely highlight to you the severe lack of common sense and humanity that your average screw had, let alone the basic inability to assess a situation and react appropriately. Most were unable to make any decisions that involved deviating from the textbook method of dealing with an incident, especially when they were confronted with two incidents to deal with at the same time.

Instead of allowing Dave to remain outside his cell with Ronnie to comfort him while they awaited the arrival of the paramedics, they insisted he return to his cell and leave Ronnie lying on the floor in the middle of the spur. It is a fact that many officers hated Ronnie with a passion and Dave realised that they would love the chance to watch him suffer and die on the floor of the

Unit that day, so there was no way he was willingly going to return to his cell and allow this to happen.

I witnessed on many occasions throughout my career staff deliberately forgetting to give inmates medication or ignoring a cry for help or cell buzzers from inmates who were either quite ill or threatening to harm themselves. It was a well-known fact that if you had a death on your wing you were treated as something of a hero in the officers' mess, as an inmate's life was the lowest of the low to a great many screws – they were expendable.

The officers dealing with this incident showed the same disregard for Ronnie's health and their main priority was to get Dave back inside his cell. When he repeatedly refused the order to return to his cell, he was jumped, and the staff began to drag him across the floor. There was no way he was going to let go of his mate, and at one time there were six big screws dragging both him and Ronnie, as he was still gripping him firmly in his arms. The only way they managed to get Dave to release his hold was when two of them stuck their fingers into his mouth and began to pull him by his jaw back to his cell whilst also applying strokes across his back and shoulder area with their truncheons. Eventually Dave had no choice but to release his grip and he was banged up, but I still believe that he saved Ronnie's life that day by staying with him for as long as was possible, thus giving the paramedics time to arrive on the scene. This

incident caused tensions to rise within the unit, as
Ronnie was such a well-respected man.

This account reflects humanity and inhumanity in one incident. It was the first of two heart attacks I suffered in the
Unit. I thank Dave Courtney for his unswerving loyalty that
day in the face of brutality, and I thank Jim Dawkins for
shining a light on the sometimes brutal attitudes and actions
of the prison officers, and demonstrating that the violence
inside is not all one-way traffic.

To complete the above story, a female auxiliary warder
accompanied me to the hospital wing in a wheelchair, and
she became more and more distressed as we waited what
seemed ages for each set of doors to be opened.

When we finally got to the hospital she whispered to me,
'They were taking their time because they wanted you to die.
They must hate you, Ronnie.'

'They do, and I fucking hate them.'

As the Unit filled up, we started to get organised. We'd
become frustrated that although there was a brand-spanking-
new kitchen on our landing, our food was being brought
over from the main wing. By the time it had passed through
the multiple layers of USS *Enterprise* security it was cold.
This became a bigger and bigger issue in our minds, but our
complaints and moaning fell on deaf ears.

It finally went off one day, although it wasn't planned.
Sometimes it was just like this in prison. Somebody jumps
up and throws something or goes for a screw, and then you

all jump up, roaring very much like you see in the films. Like putting a Swan Vestas down a petrol can. Ronnie Easterbrook was on his feet and ripped the leg off a chair. The deputy governor of the unit entered to calm things down, but I noticed the screws had activated the locking system behind him, not realising – I hope – that their boss was inside. I pointed out to the deputy governor that he was on his own and it would take a few crucial minutes for his people to get to him. The gravity of his situation hit him. There were twelve of allegedly the most dangerous people in Britain there, and a couple of the IRA boys fancied stringing him up. I pretended I was angry with the deputy governor and started to complain about the food to keep others at bay.

'We want a toaster!' I demanded.

'And hot water,' shouted someone else.

'Give us hot food and everybody will calm down,' I called to the screws as I held the deputy governor around the neck in a benign headlock.

I wanted to end the situation quickly, as I could see a nasty situation developing. If the man was left to the mercy of the pack, they might tear him apart. The only way of saving his skin, I felt, was to make out it was a personal thing between me and him.

I could see through the glass that some screws were putting on the mufti. Shields were being raised. They couldn't risk such a senior officer getting topped in his own nick. This was about to turn into a tragedy. The deputy governor, realising I was his best hope, promised he'd try and meet our demands, and I walked him to the door. A bad, bad situation was averted, but the screws afterwards suggested I was going to be charged with holding the deputy governor hostage. The reality was I'd saved his bacon, and he knew it, and the fact I was charged with impeding an officer in the execution of his duty or some such drivel proved it to me. They should have given me a medal, but I'm glad they didn't – it might have annoyed some of the others. Instead, I was rewarded with six weeks solitary for possibly saving a deputy governor's life.

It's a funny old world. And, yes, we did get a toaster, hot water and hot food straight away. Today's prisoners don't always appreciate the battles fought and sacrifices made by those that went before them in the struggle for better conditions.

I came across the same governor again towards the end of my final sentence when I was being prepared for life on the outside at Latchmere House open prison near my home. I was working on the outside for a housebuilding company on a massive site. One morning I decided to nip over to Raynes Park for a few hours to see my family and friends, but unfortunately a screw grassed me up and said he couldn't find me anywhere on site. I protested that I was in the lofts doing some lagging, but the governor (the one I allegedly 'held hostage') used this as an excuse to have me moved to the less user-friendly Wandsworth jail.

I appealed against the charge, and Joe Pyle personally made a trip to the site to remind some people that they now remembered I was in those lofts. The charge was overturned, and my lawyer applied for me to return to Latchmere House as it was an important step in my parole and release 'journey'. The governor had the final word. He said I was a bad influence on other prisoners, and that was that. He should have been grateful for what I did for him at the Unit, but instead he was embarrassed and resentful.

One Sunday when I was in Belmarsh Unit, the governor came to see me. 'Ronnie, I wonder if you would come with me. There's a friend of yours downstairs who's in a bit of a state.'

'Who is it?'

'I can't tell you that.'

'Is this a stitch-up?'

'No, Ronnie.'

I gave him the benefit of the doubt and followed him, going through the rigmarole of changing clothes three times as I moved through the elaborate triple-security-door system. When I got to the reception room Lenny McLean was sitting there, head in his hands. He was in a distressed state, having been charged with murder following an altercation at the door of a club he was bouncing.

I'd met Lenny before at the unlicensed fights that Joe had promoted. I first got to be introduced properly one night when Joe and I were out collecting 'drinks' from clubs he had connections with, and we stopped by the Hippodrome where Lenny McLean was doing the door. Joe introduced us again. Lenny looked fearsome. He was in a white shirt that it looked like his body was going to burst out of, ripping it in the process like the Incredible Hulk. I couldn't see how any punter, any man, would risk getting into an altercation with him.

'Why doesn't he get clothes that fit him?' I whispered to Joe.

'Tell him,' Joe replied out the side of his mouth.

'You wouldn't beat Ron here in a fight, Lenny, I can tell you,' Joe said to Lenny, who looked at me with half a smile, knowing full well he'd batter me.

'Don't tell me, Joe, he's a black belt karate and all that.'

'No, Lenny, Ronnie would shoot you first.'

Joe was joking again, of course, but Lenny was a dangerous man to be making jokes with. Especially that sort.

When a screw came into the reception room this Sunday in the Unit, Lenny jumped up as if to fight him.

'Calm down, Lenny. It's OK.'

'Would Lenny like to go into the Unit with you and have some lunch?' asked the governor.

They were talking about Lenny, not to him, as if he was some strange, dangerous species that had been captured in a trap.

'Ask him,' I said.

Talk of food seemed to cheer Lenny up.

I took him to the dining area. There was a tray of sausages, and Lenny politely put just one on his plate. He was like Desperate Dan – only a cow pie complete with horns would have really satisfied him.

'Take the tray, Lenny.'

'What?'

'Take the whole tray.'

Lenny took the tray with around a dozen sausages in it, grinning like a naughty schoolboy, and I picked up a tray of roast potatoes and we went chuckling away to my cell, where we had a feast. Lenny eased up then, and I told him that, from what he'd told me, the murder charge would get chucked. When it emerged that police had also laid hands on this unfortunate punter, Lenny's charges were scaled down to manslaughter and finally grievous bodily harm. He eventually got a Not Guilty at the Old Bailey.

Another chap that came in while I was in the Unit was Jack Whomes. Jack, along with his friend Michael Steele, had been convicted of the so-called Essex Boys murders. This was when three Essex villains – Pat Tate, Tony Tucker and Craig Rolfe – were possibly lured to a meet deep in the Essex countryside and gunned down with a pump-action shotgun in their Range Rover. The case captured the public imagination and has refused to budge ever since. I've never worked out why. Gangland murders and contract killings happen all the time, many unsolved and more curious than this. But the Essex Boys murders have spawned nearly as many books, dramatisations and documentaries as the Kray twins themselves.

Jack Whomes always protested his innocence, and I for one believed him. He's out now after serving a twenty-plus. He probably doesn't want to waste whatever time he has left clearing his name. He didn't speak much to me about his case, but a villain knows, and my gut feeling was here was a man who wasn't capable of killing. He was a ducker and diver. No mug, but no cold-blooded murderer either. He was in the wrong place in Belmarsh, with plenty of cold-blooded killers. I know nothing much about the case and don't have any inside knowledge, but I'd lay money that Jack had nothing to do with the triple killing. If you did a line-up for me of ten men, and one was an underworld executioner, I'd pick him out. Guarantee it. It's in the eyes and the face. They can hide it behind smiles and such, but not from one of their own.

I was eventually downgraded to just an A Category prisoner. I knew plenty in Wandsworth, but the profile was slightly younger and most were serving shorter sentences. A young fella came in and was in the cell at the bottom of my strip. I noticed him, but we didn't talk. I might have nodded to him in the dinner queue, that's all. He told one of the others that he worked for a well-known crime family, and he was in on drug charges. The 'well-known crime family' claim is common in prison, especially among younger inmates, who think by saying this they gain kudos or protection. If he really did enjoy these connections and protections, he wouldn't need to say it. People would know.

One day the head of security popped his head in my cell and asked, 'You fallen out with anyone, Ron?'

'Not me, guv. I get on with everyone, you know that.'

The officer turned to go.

'You can't leave me in suspense, guvnor. Come on, spill the beans.'

'Well,' he said, 'the kid in the patches. The yellow stripes. We spun his cell and found a toilet brush with the head snapped off and sharpened to a point. Nasty little blade. Well, we questioned him, and he said, "You know that Ronnie Field, it's for him."'

'I never asked him to do it. I ain't spoken to him. Don't know the geezer.'

'No, Ronnie. You've got the wrong end of the stick. He meant he was going to do you with it. He's made the tool to shank you.'

'Why?'

'He wouldn't say. I reckon he thinks if he plunges you that bungs him up the hierarchy.'

'What did you tell him?'

'We told him the truth, Ron.'

'What's that?'

'That if he so much as scratched you, he'd surely be dead by the end of the week.'

The boy was gone the next day and I never found out anything else. One of the mysteries of prison life.

Another time I was in the queue to use the telephone. I never pushed in. I don't know why but I clocked a geezer moving up the queue. He *was* pushing in and then stopping and then moving forward again. Something didn't seem right. He hadn't been inside long, but he wasn't someone I'd spoken to. He got behind me and I turned to face him. He'd been holding another toilet brush-adapted blade behind his back, which explained why the other prisoners didn't protest as he'd moved up the queue. The idiot brandished his weapon in my direction, but his moment had gone. And so had his bottle.

'Do yourself a favour. Throw that thing away and fuck off because I'll take it off you and stick it up your arse so hard, they'll have to take your teeth out to get the fucker out.'

The man dropped the offensive weapon and skulked off. He was promptly moved on, and I never found out what beef he had with me or what he was trying to achieve. I wasn't really bothered. It did remind me, though, to watch my back. Literally.

It happened again when I was in Wandsworth as my sentence was ending. We were separated from other units by big iron gates. I heard somebody calling me over to the gate at the end of the wing. I recognised him as a heroin dealer who Joe had fucked off on the outside.

'Come here, Ron. Wanna chat with you.'

I moved a bit closer.

'Don't think we have anything to chat about.'

'Come here, I can't hear you properly.'

He was beckoning me and smiling, taking a couple of steps back from the gate himself as if to give me more room.

'Nah,' I said, shaking my head knowingly.

'You cunt,' he hissed.

We stood looking at one another for a minute and then he dropped his arms by his side.

'Shame. I had this for you.'

From his trousers he pulled another sharp implement. I can only assume that this one was an intended revenge attack for the brush with Joe; I'd had no dealings with the man. I heard a couple of years later that he died, on the outside, from lead poisoning.

One morning around this time a couple of security officers came to my cell accompanied by a prison officer.

'We've come to take you to Wimbledon Magistrates' Court,' said one of the men.

'Really? Why's that?' I replied.

'To face charges for the theft of an electric lawnmower from a garden shed.'

I looked over their shoulders to see if Jeremy Beadle was lurking behind.

'You got the wrong bloke, lads,' I said. 'When did this happen?'

One of the guards thumbed through a sheath of paper on his clipboard.

'May 18th.'

'Which year?'

'This year.'

'This year?' I was laughing now. 'I've been inside for a good while, mate.'

I don't know if these two were mentally challenged and thought I was geeing them up, but they said, 'Come this way, Mr Field.'

Well, a trip down to Wimbledon would be a nice change, I thought, so I protested no more and went with them. Why the screws who knew me didn't pick up on it I'll never know. How delightful it was to sit in the van and drink in the scenery on the short ride from Wandsworth to Wimbledon.

At the court I was led inside, cuffed to these two clowns. The charges were read out to me.

'How do you plead?'

'Not guilty, sir. I have a very tight alibi. It can't be me as I've been in prison for the past few years.'

The magistrate was perplexed and there was much whispering from the bench. Slowly, they began to realise they had the wrong man. The wrong Ronald Field. The court blamed the officers. The officers blamed the computer. Then, when the penny finally dropped I was not the notorious Wimbledon Flymo Thief, they started to wonder who I actually was. A few phone calls back and forth from Wandsworth Prison soon made the picture clearer. Prison officers and armed police arrived, as did a bigger, more secure van. I was bundled out the building unceremoniously, as if I'd set the whole caper up and this was some impertinent escape ruse. Four motorcycle outriders were posted at each corner of the van and we set off back to the prison. Shoppers and commuters stopped and stared.

In a cell in Wandsworth, I pictured a man who had a history of rifling garden sheds and a name like mine wondering when the guards were going to turn up to take him to court. There was a helicopter up that day – I don't know if it was for me, but I wouldn't be surprised. Police love their helicopters. They're their special toys, and they just can't wait to get them up in the air. When you see them hovering high in the sky, it's likely they're not tracking some dangerous and desperate criminal but looking for Mrs Jones's missing tabby cat or a lawnmower thief.

Soon after, I regained my freedom. I vowed to enjoy myself and keep out of prison. Not by rejecting a life of crime, but doubly resolving not to get collared. The Krays came back into my life. This time it wasn't Ron or Reg, but older brother Charlie. The sensible one.

14

CHARLIE AND THE CHARLIE

I had a busy social life to finance when I was out in the mid-1990s. Charlie Kray had moved down my neck of the woods and was living in Sanderstead, Surrey. We reconnected and got busy socialising. Charlie knew what I did but would never dream of getting involved. In his mind he'd done a lump for something he didn't do; he wasn't going to do another stretch for something he *did* do. And he knew even if he was that way inclined, with his name it would be hard to go to work and people keep quiet about it.

I sometimes wondered if the name Kray had something to do with how people reacted to them. I don't mean their reputation, I mean the actual name Kray, K-R-A-Y. It has an edge to it. A Russian tinge, perhaps? Could be a name from the imagination of Charles Dickens or the pen of Ian Fleming. Would the Kray legend be so potent if they were simply Ronnie and Reggie Perkins, for example?

Charlie was the oldest swinger in town. Going out on the razzle with him was never dull. He knew every club, every manager, every commissionaire, every doorman. His celebrity and genuine charm opened almost any door. The name Kray prevented him from building up the legitimate businesses he would have preferred, and by this time I think he thought, *Fuck it, I might as well milk this Kraymania phenomenon*, and he did.

One night we went to Annabel's, a fashionable club in Berkeley Square. It was in the basement of the Clermont Club, the private members' up-market gambling den founded by John Aspinall – the original Tiger King – that was famous for being the venue where Lord Lucan gambled away his and other people's money before he committed a murder and did a runner. Since the 1960s Annabel's had been the place that people like the Beatles, Mick Jagger and George Best would hang out. On this particular night me and Charlie were being held at the door a little bit longer than usual. The manager, who Charlie knew well, appeared, brow furrowed, looking troubled.

'I'm very sorry, Charlie, but you can't come in tonight.'

'Why? What's wrong?'

The manager looked over his shoulder and leant into Charlie, hand cupped over his mouth.

'Princess Diana's inside,' he whispered, so no reporters or paparazzi could hear.

Charlie broke into a broad smile and put his arm around the manager.

'Oh, that's all right, I don't mind at all.'

The manager looked at Charlie, puzzled. It hadn't occurred

to Charlie that a paparazzi shot of the Princess of Wales having a one to one with a Kray brother would be a public relations disaster for the royal family and a major result for the tabloid press. You can imagine the headline: PRINCESS DI CLUBBING WITH CHARLES (BUT NOT THAT ONE!). The manager hailed a driver and his limo, telling him to take us around to some other clubs and get our drinks bills put on his account as an apology for our inconvenience.

Another time we had comedian Bernard Manning as the entertainment at a do for Joe's birthday. He had a reputation for not taking any prisoners, and would often alight on people in the audience and rip the piss out of them. After the show we were taken to be introduced to him, Charlie, Joe and me.

'I wondered why my manager said to me be careful who you insult and take the mickey out of tonight,' laughed Bernard.

The three of us went to the Stringfellows nightclub one evening. The club was the talk of the town – excuse the pun – and everybody wanted to be seen there. We were shown to a table and presented with a couple of bottles of champagne 'on the house'. The owner Peter Stringfellow, a familiar face on the television with his open shirt, swinging medallions and trademark mullet hairdo, walked past nearby. Joe beckoned him over.

'Peter, Peter,' he said, shaking his head.

'What's up, Joe?' beamed Peter Stringfellow, tossing his mane of luxurious curly hair.

'Peter, you know better than this … we don't drink this shit,' said Joe, pointing to an empty house champagne bottle that contrary to Joe's statement we *had* actually drunk.

It tasted like tap water, and it probably was. Peter Stringfellow couldn't apologise more, and the table was quickly loaded up with some bottles of decent authentic crystal bubbly.

Joe was invited to many social events, and I was often included. I remember going to a country club as the personal guests of the singing duo Peters and Lee. Years before they'd won Hughie Green's *Opportunity Knocks* on television and gone to number one in the charts with their song 'Welcome Home'. Lennie Peters was blind and seemed to know plenty of the chaps. We were sitting enjoying the acts when Jess Conrad came to join us. He'd been on stage earlier singing his hit. I'd never met him before, but he gave me a hug not unlike how Eric Morecambe would embrace Ernie Wise. I didn't mind that, but he kept his arm wrapped around me as he chatted to Joe.

'Tell him to move his arm, Joe, before I break it,' I whispered in Joe's ear.

'Best let him go, Jess,' smiled Joe. 'He doesn't react well to affection.'

Jess was unperturbed, removed his arm, and directed his sparkling teeth and smile elsewhere.

I have to confess I don't remember Jess as a pop star, even though he was my era. However, I do remember him in an excellent film that chimed with me at the time. It was called *The Boys* and was about a group of aimless juvenile delinquent Teds who end up killing a man in the course of a robbery. Jess and Dudley Sutton were both very good in that.

While Joe was still in prison, I was going out with Charlie regular. London, Raynes Park, Croydon, wherever. He still had plenty of energy for a man his age, enjoyed a good drink and loved a fag. In June 1996 he invited me and Bobby Gould to an evening's entertainment at the Mermaid Theatre in London, where the proceeds were to be donated to the hospice that had cared for Charlie's adult son Gary, who'd recently very tragically died following a long illness. It was an evening that would change all our lives, but we wouldn't realise it for a while.

Gary Kray was the only son of Charlie and his wife Dolly. Back in 1973 Dolly had become the unwilling lead story in the tabloid newspapers, and it would have been painful reading for Charlie too while he was still serving his original sentence for his alleged part in the McVitie murder. The previous year the house belonging to the owners of the Barn Restaurant in Braintree had been raided by two armed men, who ended up gratuitously shooting the owner Robert Patience, his wife Muriel and their young adult daughter Beverley. Robert miraculously survived a bullet to his head and his daughter a shot to the back, but Muriel succumbed a few days later to her head injuries. It was a callous home-invasion murder that shocked the nation. Some likened it to the terrible Kansas murders of the Clutter family in 1959, famously dramatised by Truman Capote in his novel *In Cold Blood* and later filmed.

Police arrested known armed robber George Ince for the murder and attempted murders, apparently acting on a tip-off. He'd given himself up when he heard he was wanted, and to his horror both Robert Patience and his daughter picked him out at an identification parade. George passionately protested his innocence. He had an alibi, he said, but wouldn't reveal it. In May 1973 he stood trial at Chelmsford Crown Court before Mr Justice Stevenson on a number of charges, including murder and attempted murder. As a QC, Stevenson had unsuccessfully defended Ruth Ellis, the last woman to hang in Britain, and unsuccessfully prosecuted Dr John Bodkin Adams – possibly the Dr Harold Shipman of his day – for murder. During the proceedings in Chelmsford, George fired his defence team and demanded that Stevenson be removed for being biased and rude. George turned his back on the judge for the rest of the trial. I guess that didn't help his cause.

The jury couldn't reach a verdict and a retrial was ordered. George, now desperate, finally disclosed his alibi to the police. He'd been having a long-term affair with Dolly Kray and had spent the night with her at the Kray marital home. His reluctance to say this earlier was well founded. He feared retribution from the Kray family as much as he did a wrongful conviction for murder and spending the rest of his life in prison.

Dolly went to visit Charlie in prison so she could tell him the whole truth, not the tabloids' version. Charlie's reaction shocked everyone, and is a testament to his genuine decency in my opinion: he told his wife she should go to court and give evidence for George. To tell the whole truth. Charlie's view was that an innocent man shouldn't spend his life in prison for a murder he didn't commit, whatever personal damage he'd wreaked on his marriage.

George Ince was acquitted, and his innocence confirmed later when two apparently unconnected criminals admitted to the shootings after getting off their canisters on drink and drugs. They'd heard there was ten grand on the premises, but only got away with a meagre £90 on the night. George and Dolly later married.

Back to the Mermaid Theatre. First, let me introduce Bobby Gould. He's not to be confused with Bobby Gould, the former Arsenal footballer and manager of Wimbledon FC, who I never went to work with. Joe put us together originally when Bobby had been to see him to seek help when some heavies had tried to muscle in on a long-firm scam he had going.

Long firms are companies that set up and buy stock, pay for it a couple of times, and when confidence and trust have been built, make a bigger order on tick, pack up and go home, having sold the stock through bent channels and pocketed the money. I went over to where Bobby was working on the day he was expecting a visit. I sat at a table with a briefcase in front of me, and when the men walked in I said

I was pleased to meet them and how much did they want. They said an amount, and I flicked open the briefcase and spun it around so they could see inside.

'Will this do?'

'Whooa!' they gasped, and stepped backwards, making the surrender sign when they saw the powerful gun inside.

'Joey Pyle says fuck off and don't come back.'

Later Bobby gave me a white Mercedes by way of thanks and we became great friends, often going out as foursomes with our partners. I helped Bobby unload his moody stock, and we grew to really trust and like one another.

Back again to the Mermaid Theatre at Blackfriars, where actor Brian Hall compered. He was most famous as the cook in *Fawlty Towers*, but he also played villains and fittingly was once an armed robber in *The Sweeney*. Sadly, he died of cancer not long after this night, and it was brave of him to honour the evening's engagement for Charlie while his days were numbered and he was in such pain.

After the show we were in the bar area, and Charlie beckoned for me and Bobby to go over and join him. He was in conversation with some men I didn't know. Jack was a stocky Geordie who, according to Charlie, whispering in my ear, 'runs Newcastle'. The football team, I wondered. Kenny was next, another northerner, and then Brian (not the actor), a big bear of a man. Charlie intimated they were 'faces' from the north, and they did nothing to dispel that impression. They were very well dressed in Armani suits and ties, but two of them were wearing shiny black Dr Martens-style boots rather than stylish shoes. Who goes to the trouble of getting nicely togged up and then finishing off with a pair of working boots? It made me quite cross.

'We may be able to do some business together, right, Jack?' Charlie grinned.

I didn't have the faintest idea what Charlie was on about. Him and Jack were fussing over each other like old mates. Jack seemed keen on me.

'Really pleased to meet you, Ronnie. Charlie's told me all about you,' enthused big Jack, who was clearly the leader of this little firm.

I asked Charlie how long he'd known these blokes. Twenty-odd years, he said. It was a throwaway answer but a crucial one. The Dr Martens boots were playing on my mind. Policemen have an unhealthy attachment to wearing boots instead of shoes. Old habits die hard. Then I told myself it was probably a northern thing. I asked Jack if we'd met before, as I thought his face was vaguely familiar.

'You been in Armley jail, Jack?'

'No, Ronnie.'

'Parkhurst?'

'No, Ronnie.'

'I thought I might have come across you in prison years back.'

'No, not me, Ronnie.'

Jack was reticent, looking back on it. I thought he might have said, 'No, but I was in this prison or that prison or I did a little bit of bird with Charlie back in the 70s', something

245

like that. But he wasn't saying anything in case he tripped himself up.

Bobby and I went along with the laughing, backslapping and round-buying, imagining that Charlie had given them some old bullshit and was trying to wangle something that we'd find out about later. I never gave it much thought. Charlie was forever introducing people, always chasing some business, a deal. I can remember the men asking whether I knew the Sayers family in Newcastle. I didn't. It was like they were trying to impress us, throwing names around. My initial impression was that they were idiots fawning over a Kray brother. At the end of the night, as we were sorting out cabs home, a very drunk Ken launched an attack on an innocent cab driver. Jack and Brian dragged him off but not before the man had suffered a beating. I thought that was out of order and drew the conclusion that Ken was a loose cannon, a dickhead, and best kept at arm's length.

A couple of weeks later Charlie called me. He said that Jack had rung and had invited us up to Newcastle to discuss business.

'What business?' I asked. 'Why me?'

Charlie said he didn't know. I told Charlie I didn't fancy it and I was skint anyway.

'It's all paid for, Ron. We won't have to put our hands in our pockets. Jack is sending up air tickets and standing a hotel for us. Come on, Ron. Keep me company. It'll be a laugh. Who knows, we might be able to nick a few quid.'

Charlie could be persuasive, and I didn't want to let him

down. I thought perhaps Jack and co. wanted him to front up a nightclub in Newcastle or something like that.

'OK, Charlie, count me in.'

At Newcastle airport Jack and Ken met us driving a swish Range Rover. I noticed they were both wearing Dr Martens-style boots again. As if reading my doubts over their villainous credentials, Jack said he'd booked us in to a nice hotel 'out of the way', where 'no eyes are on us'. At roundabouts he made a point of going around twice. Making sure we weren't being followed by the police, Jack claimed. In hindsight they were putting a lot of effort into showing us they were crooked and on the Old Bill's radar. I just thought this bloke had been watching too many cops and robbers' films. He even pulled into a pub car park for five minutes 'in case we were being tailed'. Thinking about it now, he was probably allowing some more time for his colleagues to set up the covert taping operation at our destination.

At the hotel me, Charlie, Jack and Ken embarked on one almighty drinking session, and we were joined at various points by the fat bastard Brian, a bloke they called Deano and a lady called Lisa. One of them shook my hand and said, 'I'm pleased to meet you, Mr Kray.'

Idiot. In the back of my mind I subconsciously thought undercover police couldn't be this stupid in not knowing who was a Kray and who wasn't, and in a perverse way it helped lessen my natural suspicions about them.

The hotel staff seemed familiar with Jack, and he and Brian boasted of having been drinking with Victoria Adams from the Spice Girls earlier. Brian was necking half pints of Scotch at one stage and Ken was again paralytic, constantly suggesting that we should call up some brasses. At one point Ken gate-crashed a party of about twenty women sitting at some nearby tables. They tolerated him because he bought each one of them a drink.

Charlie pleased the company with stories of his brothers, which the northerners kept asking to hear. What was George Cornell like? Who would win in a tear-up between Ron and Reg? Ridiculous, infantile bollocks. Jack said he was gutted that he'd been introduced to Freddie Foreman at the Mermaid Theatre but not realised who he was. A villain who didn't know who Fred was? That should have been a red flag.

They seemed in awe, just like the hundreds of Kray-worshipping punters that Charlie met every week. I didn't know then what exactly Charlie told them about me, but I got the strong impression that the northern firm were looking to me as the man who delivers. Like the Man from Del Monte or the Milk Tray man.

Charlie had obviously bigged me up, and I played the part. I told them a few stories about the twins, and being banged up with famous criminals on the Isle of Wight and in the Belmarsh Unit. As the day wore on and the vodkas were sunk, I gilded the lily a bit and made some shit up to satisfy them. Brian, Jack and Kenny regularly visited the toilet to have a sniff of cocaine, or so they intimated by winking and tapping the nose. Charlie and I declined, and at the end of the night Brian and Lisa went upstairs together. I finally went up to bed when two men sat down near our table wearing trousers and shirts but with no jackets.

I said to Brian, 'I think they're Old Bill.'

Brian looked over.

'Nah, I don't think so.'

All afternoon and evening, people emboldened by drink had been coming over and asking Charlie Kray if he was Charlie Kray. It was all getting a bit blurred and over-familiar for my liking.

'How's Reggie?' they'd ask. 'Give him my best.'

As if Charlie was going to visit Reg in Wayland Prison, or wherever he was, and say, 'Oh, by the way, Reg, a bloke in a bar in Newcastle sends his regards.'

'Oh yeah, what colour hair did he have?'

'Black.'

'Nah, don't know him.'

The following morning we drifted into breakfast nursing mammoth hangovers. We agreed to reconvene in the afternoon to discuss business when we felt a bit better, and I suggested my room. Jack offered his instead. When we were alone, I asked Charlie what business we were discussing. Charlie said he'd told them we could get cocaine. We could. We didn't deal in it, but we knew people that did. He suggested we do a deal with them, take some off the top and then fuck them off. Say we cannot get any more. Say we think we're being watched or something.

In Jack's statement I'd see later, he said that when we got into the room I went around and closed the windows and turned the TV volume up to limit surveillance opportunities. I did, but what he neglects to mention is that he signalled for me to do that. We sat down, and Jack and Charlie got straight to the point.

'How much can you do us a week?'

'How much do you want?'

'Five kilos a week?'

'More if you want,' shrugs Charlie.

I nearly gagged on my coffee. That was £160,000 worth of charlie a week. Over £8m a year. It was utter bullshit. Charlie knew it, I knew it and I think they knew it. This was Pablo Escobar territory. I was thinking we'd be discussing a one-off transaction for about £25k tops. I could read Charlie's mind, though. He was banking on taking the down payment off these clowns and then ducking out. He didn't fear comebacks from them, as Charlie thought they clearly believed that he was now running the Kray firm and they'd swallow the hit. Take it on the chin.

'When can you do first delivery?'

'A week or so.'

Thanks, Charlie. Later, when we were alone, Charlie asked if we could get the first five kilos. I told him I'd try, but it was a big ask. It was at this point Bobby became involved and we tried to set up a deal locally. Meanwhile, the Newcastle firm were on Charlie's case and Charlie was on mine. I used a couple of phone boxes outside Sutton railway station from where I called Jack and he called me. I made excuse after excuse, and Jack was becoming increasingly persistent and frustrated. I think he felt the deal – or more accurately the sting – was slipping away.

Finally, someone contacted me who said they could supply me two kilos only, at short notice. For all I know that offer was set up by undercover Old Bill too. The offer came via a phone call in Winners wine bar. I don't know, but what makes me suspicious is that we were given the two kilos on tick. How many people let you take £64,000 worth of product off your hands on a 'we'll pay you later' basis? Especially somebody you don't know. We told Charlie we could only get two kilos, and this satisfied Jack, to get the relationship moving. We were paying £32,000 a kilo and were going to charge Jack £36,000, meaning a £8,000 profit on the whole deal, which we were going to divvy up equally between Charlie, Bobby and me – £2.6k each. That was it. Job done. Over and out. Fuck the Geordies. I was going to facilitate this deal but no more after. It wasn't my game, but Charlie may have had different aspirations.

We first arranged a meet at the Selsdon Park Hotel near Croydon, but we couldn't make the exchange for various reasons. At that meeting at Selsdon Jack asked me if I could get hold of the 'brown stuff'.

'Brown stuff?'

'Heroin. Smack.'

'No,' I said firmly. 'I don't approve of people dealing in smack.'

'Sorry. Just asking. No offence meant.'

Jack knew the two kilos wasn't a massive amount in the

scheme of things, and was hoping that the supply of heroin would serve their treacherous purpose better.

At this meeting we dined. Bobby and I declined at first, saying we'd no money and were financially embarrassed, which was true. Brian gave Bobby £100 and Jack slipped me the same. If you think about the cash they bunged Charlie too, can you really believe they truly thought we were big-time drug dealers putting together one of the largest trades in the UK? And isn't supplying suspects with the means to help them commit a crime against the spirit, if not the letter, of the law?

We arranged to meet at the Swallow Hotel in Waltham Abbey the following week to execute the transaction. Bobby and I sat at a table, with the cocaine in a large Jiffy bag between my legs. Jack and Brian walked in.

'You got the gear?' asked Jack.

'Yes,' I said.

'At last,' grinned fat Brian. He seemed as happy as he'd been when he disappeared up the stairs with the girl.

'Where?'

I pointed under the table, and Jack bent down to look and stretched out his arm to touch it. I went as if to pull a gun from my sock. Jack jumped back, alarmed.

'Only joking,' I laughed. 'Got the money?'

'There is no money. We've had you over,' grinned Jack.

I went for my imaginary gun again. We all chuckled. It was an impressive double-bluff on Jack's part. Jack said the money was in the boot of his car in a hold-all. We went into the car park where the exchange happened – boot to boot. They even went as far as tasting the gear, like they were experts.

Bobby and I, pleased with our day's work, got into the motor and headed towards home. *That was easy*, we stupidly thought. This time we weren't fleeing the scene of an armed robbery. We'd no reason to believe things were going to come on top. Bobby ran out of cigarettes and asked me to pull into a petrol garage. He went inside, and as he came out and walked back to the car across the forecourt, armed police swooped in from all sides. We'd obviously been followed.

Guns raised and aimed, they shouted in case we were in doubt, 'Armed police, show me your hands.'

Bobby and I showed them our hands. Reading police statements later, I note the Old Bill were carrying, among other firearms, Glock 9mm SLPs and Heckler & Koch 9mm carbines.

'On the floor!' they cried.

'Not here, mate,' I said. 'There's a load of oil there. I'll lie down over there.'

I didn't want to ruin my clothes, even though it was likely now I wouldn't be seeing them again for a while.

'Are you mad? Get down!' they shouted.

I dropped to the floor on a cleaner patch of concrete and Dirty Harry stamped his foot on to my neck.

'Ease up, mate. Loosen them cuffs. I'm not going nowhere. When you're captured, you're captured.'

We were taken by elaborate escort to Ilford Police Station, where I was questioned during the afternoon and evening.

As usual, I went, 'No comment.' Various high-ranking police officers turned up and looked in my cell like I was some foreign dignitary on their manor, except they didn't speak or shake my hand. When they took me from one room to another, I spotted Bobby sitting at a table in a room with the door ajar. He mouthed slowly, 'Charlie's been nicked. Fit-up. Fit-up.'

Charlie nicked? Why? He hadn't touched anything. He wasn't there. A penny started to drop. Slowly.

The three of us appeared at Redbridge Magistrates' Court the next day charged with supply of two kilos of cocaine worth £63,000 and conspiracy to supply £520,000 worth of cocaine. Charlie and I were additionally charged with conspiracy to supply a thousand ecstasy tablets. I think that came from some loose talk that first drunken night in Newcastle. We were remanded in custody at the Brixton Unit, and then I was taken to Belmarsh Prison. To the Unit.

'See you, Charlie,' I said. 'Keep in touch.'

'Don't know why you say that,' replied a screw. 'He'll be joining you there shortly.'

So, aged seventy, Charlie Kray, crushed by the turn of events, was taken down to the prison within a prison to serve time with eleven other prisoners considered among the dastardliest men under lock and key. A lovely gesture when I arrived first was that the other prisoners had clubbed together and left tea, coffee, tobacco and biscuits in neat little piles outside my new cell. In the circumstances it was like receiving a Harrods hamper. Others came during the day, gifting me more baccy. It was heartwarming.

With time to kill, I questioned everything. Jack, Kenny and Brian were all Old Bill. At the hotel almost everyone was undercover police. Guests, hotel staff, gangsters, girlfriends, even the yucca plant in the corner. Was Jack really downing half pints of Scotch? Or was it ginger ale? Was that poor cab driver at the Mermaid a plant? If so, he certainly took one for the team. Was Lisa Old Bill? I didn't think so, as there was no indication she knew the police guys. But now I wasn't sure. Now it was clear why they wanted our conversation in Jack's room, not mine. It was all carefully miked up. Fucking hell, what a mess.

Before the trial there was a lot of negotiating between the legal teams, the judge, the police and us defendants. A senior police officer told me if that if I went guilty, they'd let Charlie go. That there wouldn't be much of a case against him. I agreed to this, but they didn't keep their word. My legal team also said the judge was minded to give me nine years on the understanding that I gave evidence exonerating Charlie and say it was all down to me. I'd already seen they weren't going to honour the Charlie walking 'deal'. I hadn't actually been given my nine years yet, so I thought if I put myself up for everything, I'd cop fifteen or more. I stayed guilty but refused to give evidence or speak.

My brief also revealed that Charlie hadn't known these men twenty years; he had known them barely twenty *weeks* when Bobby and I were introduced! If I'd known that I'd have been far more cautious in my actions and conversations. When Charlie said he'd known them about twenty years I had no reason to doubt him. He was around the country opening nightclubs and attending charity events quite frequently. He'd been to Gateshead, I remember him telling me, and met the footballer Paul Gascoigne's family. The twins themselves had mentioned Newcastle connections in our Parkhurst and Broadmoor chats. He was Charlie Kray. He knew everyone.

When I was writing this book, a friend showed me a tape of an associate from Manchester talking about our case and saying he'd warned Charlie that the Geordie lot were Old Bill. He didn't know, of course, but that was his instinct, and he's adamant he said that to Charlie. Why Charlie didn't take heed I can't say. All I can guess is that he felt he was so close to some serious dosh he chose not to believe it.

Also, you must remember that criminals are paranoid about undercover rozzers for good reason, and often wrongly accuse people. Me and a pal could be standing on Waterloo station, for example, and a sandwich-board man walks past proclaiming 'The End Is Nigh', and me and my mate would look at one another knowingly and nod 'Old Bill'. Still, I believe Charlie ignored his own instincts, and ultimately we all paid.

Don't get me wrong. I don't believe that Charlie went out to deceive us. Twenty days, twenty weeks, twenty years – a mere detail in Charlie's excited eyes. His streetwise radar had been rendered faulty by these men he believed to be naïve northern gangsters. He soaked up their hero-worship, but more importantly he gratefully received their lavish hospitality, their gifts and the promise of a serious few quid.

Also, very cynically, they entrapped Charlie – and then us – at a very low ebb in his life. Charlie's beloved son Gary had died after a torturous battle with illness in March 1995 and understandably Charlie was in bits. He never got over it. Then Ron died, and his surviving brother Reg was unwell. Charlie wasn't thinking straight, and cash-flow problems continually plagued him.

It emerged at the trial that the initial contact in this carefully planned sting was made via undercover policeman 'George' befriending Midlands-based Patsy Manning, a good old friend of Charlie's and the twins, and offering to drive him down to Gary's funeral. It wouldn't have been hard for the police to alight on Patsy. He was known around Birmingham as an old lag who'd done time with all three of the Kray brothers, and he often spoke of his close ties with the family and the firm. They even bought and read Patsy's self-published book *Crumpet All the Way*, an account of his womanising across the world. I don't think it troubled the *Sunday Times* bestseller chart.

Alarm bells should have gone off for Patsy, but who knows how long George was ingratiating himself with him? And remember that those around Charlie *knew* he wasn't a serious criminal, nor an active gangster, therefore felt no pressing need to be especially vigilant over their relationship with him. It angers me now to think of those Old Bill infiltrating

Charlie's family at that time of intense grief, raw sorrow and utter vulnerability. How low can you go?

The court heard that after Gary's funeral Charlie was invited to a party at the Elbow Room nightclub in Birmingham. It was for a friend of Charlie's called Big Albert. Charlie stayed at the Wake Green Lodge Hotel in Moseley, and he met Patsy in the bar there before moving on to the Elbow Room. With Patsy was George and his mate Deano, who was not Old Bill. Operation Acid was now in full flow. The police do love a name for their covert activities. Operation this and Operation that. I think they're competing with the Met Office with their storms in dreaming up catchier and catchier names for their projects.

Joining them later was 'Jack'. George told Charlie that Jack was a big-shot businessman from Newcastle who dabbled a bit. Charlie noticed that Jack was wearing a Rolex he thought was worth twelve grand or so. That night one of the undercover Old Bill slipped Charlie a £50 note to 'help him out'. Later Jack posted Charlie £500 to ease his cash-flow problems, and Jack and 'Brian' (there's scores of these undercover officers, I tell you) presented Charlie with a gold-plated lighter for his seventieth birthday. I believe these days they call this sort of behaviour 'grooming'.

In return for all this hospitality, Charlie invited his new generous friends down to the Mermaid Theatre in London. This is when Charlie introduced these new friends to me and Bobby. Charlie thought he was putting two parties together, and then he could walk away and wait for his cut, with limited further involvement. Jack had already by this time asked Charlie if he'd get them large quantities of cocaine, and Charlie had said he knew some men than could. That was us. Me and Bobby.

Charlie had no in-depth experience of drug-taking, importation or large-scale dealing, as far as I know, and neither did we. Cocaine had really caught on during my prison sentences, and although I saw it in pubs and clubs when I came out, and endured all the earbashing from enthusiastic users that came with it, I only took it once myself. It wasn't for me. Made me nasty. Some might say nastier than I already was.

15

TAKE HIM DOWN

The trial at Woolwich Crown Court was only part of the Establishment take-down of the last of the Krays. The media swung into action in painting this exaggerated picture of Charlie as some sort of evil crime boss presiding over his nefarious empire. He was the 'mastermind' of a scheme to 'flood Britain's streets' with £39 million worth of cocaine. It was £78 million in some papers. He was going to 'net £8 million for himself'.

The charade started with a bang at the beginning of the trial, when permission was given to the undercover officers to give their evidence behind screens through 'fear for their lives'. It was also agreed that they could reply 'Can't answer that' to any question that allegedly compromised their personal safety or jeopardised past covert work they might have undertaken, or any in the present and future. This meant that they didn't have to endure a great deal of pressure in the witness box. Hardly a fair trial.

More damaging still was the prosecution's insistence that the jury be given round-the-clock protection as there were serious concerns they were in mortal danger and could be nobbled or even murdered. This was granted by the judge. I don't believe that anybody really thought there was still a Kray gang on the outside that were capable or inclined to harm or threaten jurors. It was all manipulative theatre. *Blimey*, the jurors must have thought, *this old Kray boy must still be a dangerous gang boss if they're going to all this trouble.*

Charlie's defence was being led by Jonathan Goldberg QC, and my legal team was led by Vera Baird QC, who'd aided me way back in the Leeds trial. Goldberg had previously acted for Brian Perry in one of the Brink's-Mat trials. Brian got nine years, and sadly when he was released he was taken out by a hitman. Goldberg wasn't happy about my decision not to give evidence, following my legal advice, and had me subpoenaed. I was taken through the tunnel that led from the prison to the court. I answered 'I have nothing to say' to every question. I could see 'Mad' Frankie Fraser up in the public gallery glaring down at me. I'd soon realise why he was there.

The key plank to Goldberg's defence strategy was that Charlie was a doddering old fool, living off past glories and the legend of his brothers, who was entrapped by savvy undercover police posing as wealthy drug dealers into procuring cocaine for them. Goldberg's claim was that police essentially acted as *agents provocateurs* – a role that police are forbidden to play. Although it was a dubious strategy, I could see some sense in it, but it was humiliating for Charlie, nonetheless, especially when Goldberg called Dave Courtney and

Frankie Fraser as character witnesses, who both told the court what a useless individual Charlie was. Fraser went as far as to say that Charlie didn't have the bottle to undertake the criminal activities he was accused of.

'He's a coward, but a lovely, lovely man,' Frank declared.

The now celebrity gangster couldn't resist playing to the (public) gallery when he told Jonathan Goldberg, 'He's as innocent as you are, sir,' and then turned to Judge Michael Carroll and added, 'And you an' all, my lord.' When his 'testimonial' was over, he amused the court by saying, 'This is the first time I have left a court not to be taken on to a prison.'

Dave Courtney, who was on remand in Belmarsh Unit with us, also entertained the court by claiming Charlie 'couldn't deal cards, let alone drugs'. He went on to tell the jury, 'I'd say he was a seventy-year-old has-been, except he's not even a has-been. He's never done anything. Charlie's got holes in his shoes, and he wears a £10 watch.' It would have hurt Charlie, all this, but he must have agreed to going along with Goldberg's tactics. His self-esteem was insignificant in comparison with his liberty.

Before Dave left the courtroom, he also couldn't resist a joke. 'I liaised with the chief of police, Sir Paul Condom, over Ronnie Kray's funeral,' he said, when explaining his role as a security boss.

'I think it's "Condon",' corrected Goldberg.

'Oh yeah,' grinned Dave.

Bill Murray from *The Bill* and ghost writer Robin McGibbon also appeared as character witnesses, the latter saying that Charlie was a dreamer forever coming up with hare-brained schemes. Charlie was visibly upset hearing these sentiments, even though he knew it was part of the plan. My thoughts were that Goldberg's strategy here with the character witnesses was misjudged. However, his choices were limited due to so many incriminating comments from Charlie and me on tape. It was an uphill struggle to prove the conversations were just bravado and Charlie telling these northern drug barons what they wanted to hear.

John Kelsey-Fry was prosecuting for the Crown. One of his finest professional moments was still to come. In 2007 he successfully defended the champion jockey Kieren Fallon when he was accused of race fixing. The case was thrown out at the Old Bailey. A few years later he also got Harry Redknapp and his dog Rosie off tax-evasion charges. Harry could have been looking at bird – and Rosie at secure kennels – had they been found guilty. Kelsey-Fry was a formidable opponent for Goldberg.

More misbehaviour from the undercover cops was aired at the trial. Evidence from Charlie's seventieth birthday party, which I didn't attend because I was running around south London trying to source the charlie, revealed that one of them slept with a girl unconnected to the operation that night. This was Brian. Another rozzer was 'forced' to gyrate with a belly dancer. Probably Kenny. It's a hard life undercover. Jack, leading the sting, denied in court that he knew Fat Brian was enjoying sexual relations with the girl during the operation. Lies. It was the subject of much of their boasting, but of course they didn't tape that – or if they did, they got rid. In the witness box, Fat Brian himself denied having relations with the girl, despite having sworn on the Bible.

What we thought and hoped might be a pivotal point in the trial was when the lady in question was persuaded to give evidence. She testified that she'd slept with Brian at her Birmingham home and at a hotel where he told her he was doing a cocaine deal with the famous Charlie Kray and had £63,000 in notes in the boot of his car. She also gave evidence that Brian had asked her if she knew anyone who could supply him with five kilograms of cocaine. Was he trying to source the cocaine he had ordered from us from her? The lady said Brian had come to her family home where she lived with her three young children and had given them pocket money in the morning. She raised a laugh when asked to describe Brian's body, replying, 'Well, he's fat.'

'I liked him,' she reflected. 'We spent two weeks together. He said he was divorced and had two children. It would have been nice if it was true.'

Her evidence was assured and believable. She had no dog in the race. We hoped the jury would now see the operation for what it was following this lady's testimony. The police were dangerously indiscreet, Brian's comments to the lady potentially undermining the whole sting. They used the operation to get pissed and snort the coke they were trying to rid the streets of, they casually bedded what women they could and had lied under oath about the sexual relations with the lady. Who'd believe them about anything else?

Much of the incriminating evidence from the undercover cops related to the evening of Gary Kray's tribute night at the Mermaid Theatre, where conveniently the court only had the police's verbal word – no tape recordings. Jack reckoned I referred to 'a big one due via the north', supposedly about a drug delivery. Utter lies.

It was that wanker Jack who kept on talking about 'the Dam' (Amsterdam) and implying he had a drug chain in operation from there, although it had been disrupted because 'his man' had been 'topped'. He also gabbled on about controlling pubs and clubs in Newcastle, while asking whether there was anything down in London he could get involved with. He kept trying to get Ken to back him up: 'Didn't he, Ken?' 'That's right, ain't it, Ken?' 'Remember that, Ken?' I recall that Mermaid evening well. I wasn't pissed and just thought the bloke was a wannabe tough-guy gangster, probably on gear, talking bollocks. I met people like this frequently. Harmless, but annoying nonetheless.

They said I boasted about killing someone. If that was true, why didn't they ever question me about it after I was in custody? Someone describes committing a murder – according to them – and there's no follow-up? What does that tell you? There was no murder and no claim of murder.

'I can give you as many as you can sell,' I'm alleged to have said when asked about the supply of ecstasy tablets.

I knew more about quantum physics than I did E's. I wasn't involved in drugs as a seller or a user, and if I had been wouldn't the police have produced some back story to give this wild claim some credibility? They threw it in there to muddy the waters, to influence the jury against us. Shortly before all this, a young girl in Basildon named Leah Betts had tragically died after taking a dodgy ecstasy tablet. For a period afterwards ecstasy dealers were the lowest of the low, and a new newspaper-fuelled moral panic ensued. The afore-mentioned Essex Boys murders were sometimes linked in the press to Leah Betts. The undercover police threw everything they could into the jury's lucky-dip bucket of suspicion, hoping that some of it would stick.

A strange and sad interlude in the trial was when Charlie revealed that his brother Ron had been buried without his brain. Apparently, Home Office pathologists had removed it for analysis without family permission. When the family protested, Ron's brain was returned in a casket and a second ceremony was performed to bury it. The papers treated this as a joke, but it was a diabolical liberty and in my mind an Establishment ruse to humiliate Ron in death.

In the end, Goldberg's defence of Charlie – that police were acting as *agents provocateurs* – didn't convince the jury. I have seen the official instructions issued to undercover officers:

A police officer must not act as an 'agent provocateur'. This means he must not: incite nor procure ... a person, nor through that person anybody else ... to commit an offence, nor an offence of a more serious character, which that person would not have otherwise committed.

For the life of me I cannot see how those twelve good men (and women) and true were unable to see that the case was awash with incitement, entrapment and procurement. You couldn't move for it.

I'm surprised the operation was ever officially approved, as the Metropolitan Police had only recently come under intense scrutiny and criticism for their honeytrap operation to snare Colin Stagg, the man they were convinced had murdered a lady called Rachel Nickell on Wimbledon Common in front of her three-year-old child. With no forensic evidence to link him to the crime, the police resorted to having an undercover female officer befriend him, claim she was into satanic sadism, encourage him to confess to the violent slaying and provide gory detail that only the murderer would know.

Stagg couldn't do this, as he hadn't committed the crime. Another man, Robert Napper, was proved to be the killer some time later. The judge at Stagg's trial ruled that 'excessive zeal' had been used to incriminate the suspect, branded police efforts 'deceptive conduct of the grossest kind' and added that the whole operation was reprehensible. Maybe I'm the only one that sees the parallels with our case.

Charlie was sentenced to twelve years, I got the nine I'd been told I'd get and Bobby got five. With the time he'd served on remand deducted and good behaviour, Wobbly Bob, as we called him, would be out in two. He got out on first parole. Good on him. We called him Wobbly because he liked to dance and jog around when he'd had a drink and was happy. He said he felt guilty about getting such a small sentence compared with me and Charlie. We told him not to be so stupid, do his bird and get on with his life. On the outside we later met up and had some great times together. Bob inherited from his parents, went a bit haywire living the high life and sadly died prematurely. Wobbly Bob was one of the funnier, nicer people in my life.

That's one thing I've noticed as I've got older – inheritances can be a double-edged sword. Seen it a few times where mates have come into money, normally from the sale of the parents' gaff, and they start doing things to excess, but this time they're in middle or early old age and the constitution can't take it.

Charlie and I appealed to the High Court against the severity of our sentences, and were given the nod by our lawyers that Charlie would be reduced to a nine and me to a seven. But when we went to hear the ruling the appeal was denied. With the best will in the world, I'd be out in four years and Charlie five. Sadly, for Charlie, that was never to be. We returned to our separate prisons and never saw one another again.

A police spokesperson told the *Mirror*:

We are relieved Charles Kray is back behind bars. We believe he's been at it for over twenty years. We have investigated him in the past but never got enough evidence. Our inquiries showed he lived comfortably for years without paying any income tax and I think that speaks for itself.

'Back behind bars'? What? After twenty years of liberty and not being convicted of jack-all, there's a real need to get this old-age pensioner off the street? 'At it'? At what, exactly? The police are deliberately vague here, as they knew they had nothing on Charlie since he came out of prison. 'Living comfortably for years without paying any income tax'? Yeah. Not as comfortably as the average detective in Scotland Yard, I'll wager. They'll be wanting to give one Derek Trotter life on this basis.

Superintendent Gavin Robertson, who headed the police operation, chimed in:

It gives me no pleasure to see a seventy-year-old man go to jail. But this is a proper reward for a very professional operation and all the hard work by my team.

'Professional operation'? Brian? Kenny? Bashing up a cab driver? Pursuing and seducing a member of the public? Who are you kidding? What a load of bollocks, the lot of it. This Mr Big who didn't own his house, or his own car, who was scratching a living, existing from day to day and was thrilled to get a present of a Ronson lighter? Propaganda and smear. Does avoiding a bit of income tax warrant destroying the man? There were other reasons. Clearly.

I firmly believe that the Establishment made a definite decision to bring Charlie Kray down, and Bobby Gould and I were collateral damage in that endeavour. The directive wouldn't have come from the police, I'm sure. Charlie wasn't running any criminal empire; he wasn't responsible for a drug ring or any other ring, for that matter. Their surveillance of him would have confirmed that. His lack of money and assets told its own story.

I can imagine the conversation.

Someone very high up: We need to bang this Charlie Kray character up, and for a long time. This Kray adulation has to stop – films, books, fan clubs, TV appearances. This other brother will be on *Give Us a Clue* next.

Senior police commander: But he's not actually doing anything really criminal, sir.

Someone very high up: I'm not concerned with detail. Get him under lock and key, and do it in style.

Poor Charlie wasn't even a gangster, but the British Establishment were going to use Al Capone tactics to bring him down. The Chicago gang boss during the Prohibition era in America was finally taken off the streets on tax evasion charges. I'm not making comparisons between Capone and Charlie – there are none. I'm saying they magicked stuff up to get Charlie, just like they did with a real gang boss in the 1930s.

The problem to them was that the Krays had become a phenomenon again and, now that lawful execution wasn't an option, it was hard to punish the twins any more than they

273

already had. The interest in them that built from the sensational newspaper and television reporting of their 1969 trial, and catapulted them to cult status after John Pearson's *The Profession of Violence* book, never really waned, and in 1990 the whole Kray admiration, hero worship and glorification thing stepped up a level with the release of the mainstream film *The Krays*. Kraymania had gone mainstream.

The movie was a big success and has become a British cult classic. The *People* splashed a story alleging that the twins made £225,000 from it, and Charlie himself was paid £85,000. I don't know if these figures are true, but the fact that the family was seen to be profiting from their historic crimes would have rattled cages in very high places. Stories coming out of Broadmoor that Ron had a butler, and from the various prisons that Reg was in that he was conducting a sprawling business empire from his cell, didn't help matters. The Establishment message that 'crime doesn't pay' was being undermined, and they can't have that.

On the back of the film and the renewed interest in the legend of the Krays, Charlie found himself in demand, appearing on TV with John McVicar in a documentary called *The Big Story*. McVicar was part of the problem as far as the Establishment was concerned. There had been a very successful film about him too, with another star from the music world, Roger Daltrey of the Who, in the lead role. Although McVicar was now a reformed character and apparently an intellectual, now clutching a pen not a gun, for some years he'd been an armed robber and successful escapee from prisons. The worry was that Daltrey had turned John McVicar from public enemy number one into a national treasure.

Frankie Fraser's celebrity star was also rising. He was entertaining punters in pubs and clubs up and down the country, and there was even talk of him and Charlie doing a tour of small theatres. Frank launched his gangland tours with Tony Lockwood, a former radio host, where they took wide-eyed members of the public around all the key spots: the Blind Beggar where George Cornell was shot, the Vallance Road childhood home of the Krays and so on. As the coach crawled around London, Frank stood in the aisle clutching his microphone and providing a running commentary. I heard that the coach driver was once so distracted by his performance that he accidentally nudged the car in front. The motorist jumped out and stormed up the steps of the coach, swearing and shouting, ready to pull the old coach driver out his seat.

'Can I help you, mister?' said Frank over the mic, turning round to face him.

The angry motorist did a double-take.

'No problem,' he replied and walked backwards out of the coach.

There was no sign of the Kray adulation abating, and when in 1993 a march was organised from Liverpool Street to Downing Street calling for the release of the twins, I expect the Kray problem floated higher up political in-trays. It was reported that the comedian Mike Reid and the actress Barbara Windsor were marching that day. Now that the general public were becoming vocal and militant in support of their heroes, the men from the ministries knew they had to do something. Ron's funeral and the massive turnout would have unsettled them even further.

Charlie was lifted by the police in connection with the murder of Donald Urquhart in 1994. Urquhart, a business-man, was shot three times in the head on Marylebone High Street by a motorcyclist while walking with his girlfriend. Charlie had nothing to do with it, and I'm sure the police knew that. He was released very quickly with a clean bill of health by the Old Bill, but not before plenty of headlines about him being questioned by detectives looking for the 'Mr Big' behind the shooting. I suspect it was all about changing public perceptions of Charlie. Two men were even-tually convicted of the murder, which was a contract killing relating to Urquhart's business interests.

In September 1995 Charlie went on *The Frank Skinner Show* on peak-time television. Skinner was a comedian, chat-show host and presenter who was pretty much at the top of his game and attracting millions of viewers on a Saturday night. The idea was for Frank to take the piss out of Charlie. That was his act. Charlie walked on to the tune of 'Getta Bloomin' Move On! (The Self-Preservation Society)', the cockney rhyming slang song from the film *The Italian Job*, and he was sat down next to some eccentric geezer who said he was the Sheriff of Nottingham.

Frank cracked a not very funny joke about cutting people's feet off, and then asked Charlie if he was guilty of disposing of Jack McVitie's body, the charge he'd got his bird for at the 1969 trial. Charlie calmly denied this and made the point that the Establishment locked him up for ten years simply for being a Kray. He said he had no hard feelings, though – it was in the past and he wanted to move forward. Despite Frank's gentle efforts to undermine him, Charlie came across as an amiable, straight-going guy. The powers that be worried he'd end up presenting *The Generation Game* next. I have a hunch that the meeting I imagined above, between someone very high up and the senior policeman, took place soon after *The Frank Skinner Show* aired.

Reg Kray phoned a radio station from Maidstone jail, got through and was put on air. He said that police had framed his elder brother in order to crucify him and kill the Kray legend once and for all. Charlie was a political prisoner, he insisted.

Charlie's barrister Jonathan Goldberg later reflected to the *Jewish Chronicle*:

Charlie Kray was the most perfect gentleman, the most beautifully mannered man. He was the charming face of the Kray brothers. Women of all ages loved him. You would have been very happy to have dinner with him. You couldn't get down to the case because he was reminiscing about 'the great characters of the East End'.

If the police really believed that Charlie was a gangster or a drugs baron or a mastermind of various criminal enterprises, why didn't they tap his phone? Maybe they did and there was nothing on there. Or maybe they didn't because they knew they'd find nothing, and that wouldn't help the case. Why didn't they tap my phone? Remember they were supposed to believe I was able to easily supply cocaine to the value of £38 million, which would make me one of the biggest suppliers in Europe!

And if their objective really was to reduce crime and banish drugs from our streets, why didn't they pursue the onward chain they'd supposedly uncovered? By getting to my source, they'd be closing in on a big chunk of the UK supply. They didn't because they never believed I could source that volume of cocaine; and also, they didn't want to complicate a venture that was purely designed to bring Charlie Kray down and so deliver a fatal blow to the Kray movement. The Krays must not prevail, at any cost.

At the end of the day, undercover police sought out Charlie Kray, they groomed him with hospitality and gifts, they asked him to supply drugs that did not exist, they persisted when he couldn't deliver the sort of amounts they needed for a decent conviction and they might even have supplied them to him (me) for delivery back to them. If that doesn't constitute entrapment, and if the police weren't acting as *agents provocateurs*, I don't know what does.

EPILOGUE

I'd spent my fiftieth birthday on remand, and now I was looking at not being released again into society until I was closing in on sixty years of age. It was time for reflection. Even armed robbers have to retire. I decided to knuckle down and do my bird peacefully, jumping through the hoops they put in front of me and saying the things they wanted to hear to make sure I motored towards my earliest possible parole dates. I did the courses they requested and recommended, and was generally a good prisoner. This time I wanted to get out and stay out.

My final bit of porridge was in Ford Prison in Sussex. I'd descended the category ladder and this open prison was my last stop before being freed. 'Open prison' is a contradiction in terms. I mean, if it's open and you can walk in and out, it's not really a prison, is it? I met some nice people in there, but there were a few idiots too. I witnessed at least two people scale the fence to escape when they could have just walked out the fucking gate.

There were different sorts of criminals in there, fraudsters and bent police particularly. I remember three Old Bill came to my table one lunchtime and went to sit down.

'You can't sit there,' I said.

'There's three empty spaces,' replied one.

'I don't care if there's ten empty spaces, you're not sitting at a table with me.'

They shrugged and went elsewhere, but I wasn't having it. I know we're all criminals, but you don't get much lower than bent rozzers. The lowest of the low, almost.

I didn't even serve a year in Ford. In 2003 I was let out. My pal Kevin picked me up once more. This time he was in a Smart car. The Rolls-Royce days were over, seemingly.

'What the fuck is this?'

'It's a Smart car,' Kev says.

'Let's hope the wind doesn't blow us in the sea, then.'

But I was pleased to see when I squeezed in that a bottle of Smirnoff, a bottle of tonic and a bottle of champagne were jutting out the ice bucket on the back seat.

We headed straight for Joe Pyle's place. Joe had been released from his sentence just as I was going in. I'd seen him not long before on home leave, but it was great to be together, knowing nobody had to report back to any jail. Joe's kitchen – Pyle HQ – was the place to be. Later, Big Harry had sorted a coming-out party at Winners wine bar for me, and as usual the boys gave me a nice drink to tide me over. I first met H in Parkhurst, years before, where he was serving time for armed robbery. I was in Highdown jail one time with Harry, and I remember the police – that's who they said they were – came in the middle of the night and took him to Epsom Downs, where they threatened to shoot him if he didn't spill the beans on some south London criminal business. Needless to say, no beans were spilt.

I met Wally Stockins in Highdown. He was a small but tough gypsy man who'd been a professional boxer and bare-knuckle fighter in his time. Joe Pyle knew him and his brother Jimmy Stockins well, and gave them a good name. Joe said Jim was up there with the toughest prize fighters he'd ever known and that the brothers were as loyal as they come. One day Wally was in the serving area complaining loudly about the meagre portions of meat he was receiving. The next day I removed a freshly killed mouse from a trap and placed it on a plate with the lid on top and asked one of the servers to dish it up to Wally.

'What the fuck!' exclaimed Wally as he lifted the lid.

'You wanted more meat, Wall,' I said, and we all had a good laugh.

I got to know Wally better on the outside, and met his brother Jim and their younger cousin Joe Smith. Joe was also a bare-knuckle fighting man, but in an unusual career move took up golf and attained professional status. We've enjoyed many good times together.

My siblings had started dying, cancer galloping through them without mercy. Billy went first, then Ted, Peter, Dalla and finally Pat all sadly followed in quick succession. As I write, only Cissy remains. I maintained good relations with all of them in adulthood, becoming closer again as we aged. They all knew what I did for a living, and the precarious and violent life I led. I was the only sibling to choose crime as my career, and to my knowledge none of them stepped over the threshold of a police station involuntarily. That's not to say they weren't scarred by our childhood. They were. But they never commented or passed judgement on me. We were from a generation that believed someone's business was their own. We rarely discussed the old days because they weren't the good old days by any measure. They were always there, though, each one of us having our own personal horrors that we didn't want to burden one another with.

Charlie Kray saw the new century in, but only just. He died in Parkhurst jail on 4 April 2000 at the age of seventy-two. I knew he wouldn't last. I remember him rolling up his trousers one day in the Unit and showing me his legs, which were black. His circulation was knackered from years of excessive smoking. He realised he had to make the age of nearly eighty to be safely out again and he knew in his heart that he wouldn't get there. The system crushed him, just as they intended.

Coincidentally, I went to see the governor about something on the day he died. I can't remember what.

'The answer is no,' he said to me as I stood in front of him and before I'd even opened my mouth.

'No, what, guvnor?'

'No, I will not grant you permission to attend Charles Kray's funeral.'

Reggie Kray was allowed out for his elder brother's funeral a few weeks later, albeit handcuffed. The crowds turned out again, to say farewell to Charlie and get a glimpse of Reggie in the flesh. Reg looked gaunt, and he was by now probably facing up to his own mortality.

'Charlie was the friendliest of people. I'm sure everyone here today would like to see everyone more friendly to each other' – this reflective comment and tribute from Reg to the press touched me. Reg was right. Charlie was a friendly man. That's how I'll remember him.

The respected crime journalist Duncan Campbell wrote an incisive obituary, which opened:

His autobiography was entitled *Me and My Brothers*, but in reality Charlie Kray always knew that it was really My Brothers and, very far behind, Me. If ever there was a man haunted by a famous family name, it was the Kray twins' elder brother. It followed him around from the 50s to his death, like a tightly fitted electronic tag.

Campbell concluded:

His funeral will not be as massive as Ronnie's – a strange event that hovered halfway between *Pulp Fiction* and *The Lavender Hill Mob* [...] His mourners – and there will be plenty – will wonder whether, without the existence of the terrible twins, people would have seen a different person, or whether the one sent down for a final stretch was the proper Charlie.

Reggie Kray died later in the same year. The authorities finally allowed him his freedom on 'compassionate grounds' when they knew his remaining life was measured in weeks, not months. His wife Roberta, who he'd married in prison a few years earlier, got him into a hotel in Norwich, near Wayland Prison, as he was in no condition to travel far, and he died there several weeks after his release. Joey Pyle, Freddie Foreman and Johnny Nash went to see him on his deathbed. It was certainly the end of an era, but if anyone thought this would herald the end of the Kray legend and the public obsession with the twins, they couldn't have been more wrong.

The amount of people that feed off the Krays even now astounds me, as does the continuing interest from people who weren't even born when the twins were at liberty. Many of these delusional fantasists wrote to Ron and Reggie in prison and because they got a reply (Ron would respond to a postcard) and even a visit decide they are 'made men'. They turn up at all the gangster funerals with more gold hung around their necks than Mark Spitz and clutching unlit cigars the size of Exocet missiles. The photographic agencies and the clueless press snap them as if they were barons of the underworld. It's a farce.

I heard from Charlie Bronson regularly after I came out from my final sentence. He used to call Joe at his house from Wakefield Prison and we'd all have a chinwag. I was sorry for him and his situation. He fanned the fame and attention that had come his way, and I can understand that – anything that helps you get through. But the more fame and attention he got, and the larger his legend grew, the less chance there was of him coming out. It was and is a vicious circle. Charlie is a talented artist, and his work has become collectable and valuable. He has kindly gifted me several of his surreal and unique drawings. I enjoyed our visits and telephone conversations, and was thrilled for him when he told me he was having a film made about his life. I was flattered when he invited me to become 'technical adviser' to the film, although I feared it wouldn't help his cause to regain his liberty.

I thought I could be handy to the film-makers in keeping an eye on authenticity, and that's how I saw my role. You see so much on television and on film about prison and criminal life, and you think this couldn't have happened and that doesn't work, and so on. Little things can ruin a viewing experience, in my mind, and they don't need to. I get particularly irked when they make unforgivable errors with clothing – putting 1960s villains in garb that wasn't worn until the 1980s, for example.

However, Charlie had a different view of what a technical adviser should be. As the momentum of the film built up, as the finance fell into place, Charlie was calling me daily. Do this. Do that. Go there. Call her. Call them. It was getting on my wick.

One day I said to him during a call, 'Charlie, I thought I was meant to be an adviser, not an errand boy.'

He wasn't happy, and sadly that was the last phone call we had together. I wish Charlie well, and hope and pray that we can meet up again, this time not confined by four grey walls. The film got made, by the way, and I was pleased to meet actor Tom Hardy at Joe's house one day. A nice man, who went on to play both Reg and Ron Kray in the film *Legend*. I thought that *Legend* was a far better film than *The Krays* and that Tom's Ronnie was uncannily accurate, considering he'd never met the man.

One day Joe asked me if I had a passport and when I said yes, he said we were flying to New York.

'What for?'

'To meet some very important people. Don't worry, it's all paid for.'

The last time somebody told me not to worry and a trip was 'all paid for' it was Charlie Kray and I ended up getting nine years.

'We'll never get into America, Joe. Not with our form.'

'Don't fret, Ronnie, it's all been taken care of. Visas, everything.'

We left from Heathrow flying into Kennedy Airport, and I was amazed to pass through domestic security. Once we were in the air Joe revealed we'd be meeting members of the Gambino crime family and others. He didn't say why, but I had no reason to doubt him as I knew he had international connections. Nice people, he said. When we landed at New

York, and passengers started to release their belts and stand to unload the overhead lockers of their hand luggage, a member of the cabin crew politely asked Joe and me to remain in our seats.

'Here we go,' I said.

Sure enough, a group of men in well-fitted suits boarded and made their way down the aisle. They took badges from their inside jacket pockets and flopped them open in front of us. Joe said later that the badges said CIA; I thought FBI, although it could have been another acronym relating to immigration. They told us we'd not be disembarking and were to remain on the airplane until it turned around to fly back to London. They weren't offering any explanation and only said we should never have been allowed to board in London in the first place. There was no negotiation to be had. They didn't even ask us the purpose of our visit. God only knows what Joe would have said to that one. Before we knew it, the cleaners were vacuuming around our feet and a whole new plane-load of passengers were boarding. So, at least I can say I've visited the United States of America. Sort of. Life with Joey Pyle was never dull, and in all the things we did together over all the years I treasure the laughs we had the most.

He fell ill a couple of years after my release. He confided in our friend Del that he feared he was suffering from lung cancer. I spent a lot of time with him at the house and in the club, and I could see he was weakening. One day he was upbeat when Del and I were round his gaff. He said he'd had good news and that the doctors had told him he was clear of cancer. He had something called motor neurone disease, though, which was a muscle-wasting disease. Joe explained that he'd get to the gym and build his muscles up. I don't know if he thought that could reverse the course of the illness or whether he was putting a brave face on it. Unfortunately, motor neurone disease is an incurable, progressive and horrible crippling condition.

I was at Joe's bedside, along with his son Young Joe, his brother Ted, and Charlie and Ronnie Richardson, in the hospice in Cheam when he died. Others were in the room adjoining. It was one of the saddest days of my life. I'd been with Joe nearly fifty years.

We didn't have any heart-to-hearts or discussed what was coming – we'd both tiptoed around it and carried on as normal. However, there was one afternoon when Joe and I were alone in his kitchen and the disease was visibly progressing.

'Ronnie, you've been staunch,' he said out of the blue.

'Thanks, Joe,' I replied.

'Staunch,' he repeated.

'And you too, Joe.'

And no more was said.

A Polish geezer called Chuck was part of the inner group, and I didn't like him at all. He was manoeuvring to take over from Joe even before the inevitable happened. He was a big lump and said he was ex-Polish special forces. One night he came into a club I sometimes used and sat on my stool. He had a gun tucked into his waistband and made no attempt to conceal it. He wanted people to see it. My loyal pal Andy Harris pinned him up against the wall, pressing his body on him so he couldn't get at the gun.

'What's going on?' I asked.

'He's got a gun and was going to get it out.'

I told him to fuck off and not come back. But he did the next day with another bloke and a driver. The club doors were locked; you needed a fob to gain entry and we told them to go over the intercom. When they didn't, Andy and I decided to go outside.

'You ain't coming in, not now, not never,' I said firmly.

'Go on, off you trot,' chipped in Andy.

'Keep out of it, you,' said Chuck. 'It's fuck-all to do with you.'

'It's everything to do with me. I'm with Ronnie.'

Andy's a few years younger than me. A big man himself, he has absolutely no fear, and his loyalty and friendship to me I value highly. I moved my hand to the inside of my jacket. I wanted them to think I was carrying, but I wasn't. The driver went to the boot, where I guess there was a shotgun stashed. Andy shook his head, and he changed his mind. Didn't see Chuck again.

I was honoured to be invited by Young Joe Pyle to be a pallbearer at his father's funeral, which he was organising with help from Dave Courtney. It was wet and overcast on the last day of February 2007, and Joe's coffin was pulled in a carriage by four glistening black horses from his house in

Lower Morden Lane to St Teresa's Church on Bishopsford Road. Members of the Outlaws Motorcycle Club cut a path ahead on their bikes for Joe's carriage, which was followed by the longest line of black funeral Mercs (twenty-seven I was told) and similar motors as far as the eye could see. Large crowds followed on foot.

Dave Courtney observed, 'At Ron Kray's funeral ninety per cent of the people gathered didn't know him. But here, at Joe Pyle's, ninety per cent of the people *do* know him.'

Dave was correct. There was the usual gangster funeral groupies and curious members of the public, but I knew the bulk of the people there – some well, some not so – and if I knew them, then Joe would have known them all much better.

I was proud to carry Joe's coffin into the church along with Young Joe, Freddie Foreman, Ronnie Nash, Roy Shaw and Jamie Foreman, Fred's actor son. After the funeral we moved on to the burial at Merton Cemetery on Garth Road. It was still pissing down, and we had to carefully navigate puddles and avoid slipping in the mud as we carried Joe from the ornate carriage to his grave. As we lowered my friend into the ground it hit me, and I wrestled with tears. Jocelyn Brown, famous for her hit 'Somebody Else's Guy', sang 'Amazing Grace', and her beautiful voice floated across the cemetery as all the mourners stood in respectful silence. The only competing noise was the uninvited black police helicopter hovering overhead trying to ruin the moment and disrupt the solemn day. If it could have shat down on all of us, it would have.

The police show of power extended to them closing most of the pubs in the area. To my knowledge the only one allowed to open was the Beverley – one of Joe's locals, and it was here the mourners drifted back to for the wake. The pub was packed with family and friends, young and old criminals, television and music stars, footballers and boxers. I stayed for a while but slipped away with a few others to a working men's club nearby, where I reflected on the day and our shared past, and toasted Joe with a large vodka and tonic.

The papers the next day were full of the funeral and Joe. The *Daily Mail* wryly commented, 'Against all the odds Joey Pyle died of natural causes.'

There was some truth in that, but what they didn't get or didn't wish to know was that Joe was a shrewd diplomat who rose above gangland squabbles. He didn't run around shooting people or shouting his mouth off in pubs and clubs. He wasn't fixated on his image and legend. He operated under the parapet and had good relations with most of the various factions in the so-called underworld. Had he had been a straight-goer he would have risen to become CEO of a large corporation, globe-trotting while tying up deals, marketing, promoting and selling, polishing the company brand. He called his autobiography *Notorious*, but I thought he should have named it *The Fixer*. Because that's what he did: he fixed up deals and he fixed things for people when they went wrong. In our world it was *Joe'll Fix It*. And he always did. There will never be another like him.

Joe raised millions of pounds for charities over his lifetime and helped hundreds of people. I know it's a tired old cliché, but Joe really didn't talk about it. One of the causes he enthusiastically supported was that of Craig Shergold, a local kid suffering with cancer. There was an appeal to send him a card to raise his spirits, and Craig became one of the first internet sensations, receiving in all an estimated 350 million cards. Carshalton Post Office were not at all happy. The money raised went towards sending Craig to America, where he had a successful operation for his cancer. He grew up and made it to early middle age, when sadly he was taken out by Covid.

Following Joe's funeral there was a meeting in a private room, where the topic of discussion was what happens next? Who, if anyone, will be stepping into Joe's shoes? Who will look after business? It was an informal chat to kick the subject of the world after Joe around. Among those present were me, Young Joe, Roy Shaw, Freddie Foreman and Johnny Nash. Someone suggested I might want to give it a try, but I knew it wasn't me. I know my limitations. And, besides, diplomacy has never been my strong point.

I lead a quiet life with my partner now, and we enjoy our children, grandchildren and friends from all walks of life. I love to chat and hear people's life stories. I see friends from my past when I can, but each year more and more names are getting crossed out the address book. Indeed, the pen is hovering over my own entry in the book. I'm sorry for the innocent people I hurt along the way, although I never intentionally hurt anyone that was innocent in my eyes.

From the miserable embers of my dark childhood came an unexpected surprise that has helped make my winter years much more comfortable and enjoyable. I consider myself a very lucky man. If anybody asks me how I am, I always reply, 'Mint condition', and that's how I feel. Mint condition. I've been blessed with a long life, whatever happens now.

I don't lose any sleep about what lies ahead. I can't change anything now. But if there is a God and he's going to judge me, then I take comfort from the fact I've got loved ones in Heaven and I've got loved ones in Hell, so I'm relaxed about wherever he sends me. Adiós, amigos.

INTERVIEW

On 29 March 2023 I visited Ronnie Field and interviewed him about the book we'd worked on together since November 2022.

MARTIN: How do you feel now you've written your life story?

RONNIE: I've thoroughly enjoyed the experience, to be honest. I thought one day I might do it, I guess. That's why I kept all those court transcripts and files I gave to you – thinking they may come in useful one day. You always wonder if your life will be interesting enough to others and when I see books coming out like *I Was Violet Kray's Milkman (For Two Weeks When Her Regular One Went Down to the Caravan at Sheppey)*, I think yes, it must be. I mean, there's no such book but there probably will be soon.

I've never opened up like this to an outsider about my childhood. I always minimised what went on, even to myself, so I found telling you very hard and sad. First of all, I was shocked at how shocked you were. I feel sorry for myself as a boy and for my siblings about what we went through. And poor old Mum. I wasn't going to say too much about those days, but it all came tumbling out. Still, there's stuff that happened to me and my brothers and sisters that I don't want to air in public. It's horrible and humiliating, and I'm not going there. My siblings have gone to their graves with those awful memories and so will I. Writing this book with you has made me think more and more about those days, and how those childhood years impacted on all of us kids. It's dawned on me that we were fortunate that one of us wasn't killed.

When I showed my sister Cissy the manuscript she had reservations, especially about revealing what poor Pat suffered at the hands of Uncle Fred, but then she said Pat isn't here now and it's an important part of the story. 'Actually,' she said, 'you make it sound better than it was.'

MARTIN: Do you feel your abusive and difficult childhood made you the man you became?

RONNIE: No. I know that's the thing these days, to blame everything on a bad childhood. But no. That cranky psychiatrist in Parkhurst asked me a similar question. 'Ronald, do you think your upbringing made you the man you are?'

'What am I? What are you implying?' I asked. I was playing with him.

'A violent criminal,' he replied.

But seriously, I became an armed robber because I wanted nice things. That's it. The things I could never have got legitimately. And once I'd had the nice things, I couldn't bear the thought of going back to a life without them. Simple as that. It became my way of life. When you've experienced desperate poverty, especially when affluence surrounds you like it did me in Cheam, you crave a different life.

MARTIN: Do you have any regrets about the life you led?

RONNIE: No.

MARTIN: Do you want to expand on that?

RONNIE: I don't know what you want me to say. I regret spending so much time in prison, and being away from my family and freedom for so many years. I regret getting caught. But I suspect that's not the answer you're looking for.

MARTIN: No, fair enough. Do you have any remorse about the people you hurt and the people you frightened?

Long pause.

RONNIE: Yes, I suppose I do. Those four people in Leeds I shot, I feel remorse about that. I didn't know them. They weren't interfering, they got in the way of a bit of work, but they didn't know they had. It was unintentional. I was shooting at a door. I'm sorry for that. Other people I hurt were mainly villains, like me. I don't have remorse about that. It could easily have been me. I guess I frightened innocent people in banks and I'm sorry for that. I didn't think about it at the time as it was a part of the job. My daughter works in a bookies and I tell her if anyone comes in with a gun, give them the money.

MARTIN: What advice would you give a young person going into crime today?

RONNIE: Don't do it. No point in robbing banks anyway – there's hardly any cash in them nowadays. In any case, CCTV and cameras have changed all the rules.

MARTIN: But if that young person was like you – had a tough upbringing and wanted nice things like you did – what advice would you give them?

RONNIE: Fraud. Go into fraud. It's profitable, cleaner. Less physically dangerous.

Martin laughs.

MARTIN: Ronnie, you're meant to deter them, not tell them what branch of crime to go into!

RONNIE: Am I? I thought you said if they were determined to enter the world of crime. It all changes so fast, Martin. The generation that came through and took over from us are probably already looking over their shoulders now. It's much more violent now. I mean, when we committed violence there was normally a reason – revenge, personal gain, defending something – but now you can get your head blown off for wandering into the wrong postcode. It's senseless. You know what, though? The world is mad these days. When I was a young man, when I walked into a bank or a post office with a mask on, people jumped out their skins. Now, if you walk into a branch without a mask on, people jump out their skins. [*Ronnie is referencing Covid practices here*]

MARTIN: Why do you think your generation of criminals from the last century fascinate the public so much, even to this day? You don't see it so much with modern criminals. Where's the twenty-first-century Bruce Reynolds, John McVicar, Freddie Foreman?

RONNIE: Rules. There was a code. It's not there now. The general public weren't in danger from us. They are now. Most of our lot never burgled anybody's gaff. None of our lot ever mugged people. We didn't hit women. Most of us didn't take drugs. We dressed well. Wouldn't be seen dead in a tracksuit or shell suit. We were polite around women. Although our business was misbehaviour, we knew how to behave. Know what I mean? Also, there's another reason with a lot of men who lap up all this true-crime stuff: they'd have liked to have been us but didn't have the bottle.

MARTIN: Do you miss it?

RONNIE: Yes, I do. I'll always miss the buzz. From the meets to plan the robbery, to staking it out (when we bothered), to the absolute fucking adrenaline rush from carrying out the blag. Counting the money afterwards, and the biggest kick of all … spending the fucker. But it's a dangerous world. Crime, I mean. There are always younger, stronger, worse men coming through, and you have to make way in the end and give it up. Know what I mean? Your brain writes cheques that your body cannot cash.

MARTIN: Do you believe in punishment? And does prison work?

RONNIE: I believe in hanging. For paedophiles and child killers. But I can see the dangers. If we had what I believe to be corrupt Old Bill, gullible juries and biased Establishment judges, innocent men would now and then get executed. Look at what happened to Derek Bentley and that poor bloke in the Christie case [*Timothy Evans*], and in this book I mention George Ince and Colin Stagg. It could have ended badly for them if they'd been born a few years earlier. But you have to have punishment, I suppose, or there would be no deterrent and everyone would be at it. Less to go round for us poor blaggers [*laughs*]. As an armed robber you knew the downside was a big lump of porridge if you got caught. We all knew the deal. And we took it without too much complaint, so we thought it was a fair risk to reward. Never thought about it too much. Does prison work? Sometimes it does, sometimes it doesn't. I've known people who went straight and changed their lives after a lump of porridge. But then there were people like me who kept coming back for more. As I just said, it's a deterrent for most of the population, so in that way it works. It's important for people to realise prison isn't full of people like Ronnie Barker and Richard Beckinsale. Far from it. It's a dangerous, nasty place, and it's worse now than it was in my day. Believe me. Don't go there, people.

MARTIN: Finally, Ronnie, do you believe in God?

RONNIE: Not sure.

MARTIN: I guess I'm saying, do you have any concerns over what happens next? In the next life, if there is one?

RONNIE: As I said in the book, I've got friends up there [*points to the ceiling*] and I've got friends down here [*points to the ground*]. I'm cool about wherever I go.

MARTIN: Thanks, Ronnie, I've really enjoyed the experience as well. When I first met you I didn't really know you, and although we'd been introduced briefly about twenty years ago and I'd heard your name over the years, I was concerned about how the book might unravel. But I believe you've led a life that few did and no one else now will. You tell your story in an insightful way, and unlike some of these true-crime books, you certainly walked the walk to be able to talk the talk. It's social history, Ronnie, and you've immersed us in a world that's fast disappearing from living memory.

RONNIE: I'll drink to that.

[*Ronnie and Martin touch glasses*]

RONNIE: Mint condition.

POSTSCRIPT

Just as we were putting the finishing touches to *Nefarious*, I had a phone call bringing me the shocking news that Dave Courtney had taken his own life. I found it so hard to take in that my first reaction was that somebody had taken him out. Something in his past had caught up with him, perhaps. It's not unusual for such things to happen in the world we inhabited. I had spoken to Dave on the phone a few days earlier and he was his usual buzzy self. He was joking, laughing and planning for the future. He'd bought and was restoring a canal boat. He was telling me how he'd been abroad to get his teeth done at considerable cost. Strange to go for all that cosmetic surgery malarky when you're planning to end your life. 'Don't forget to put me in your book,' he signed off with.

It was incomprehensible to me that he would top himself but, after speaking with his close friend Brendan and seeing and hearing about farewell videos Dave had made to his family and friends, I had to accept that he had done exactly that. What drove him to it I suppose we will never definitely know. I understand he had health issues and feared further bodily decline, but the Dave I knew was tough and resilient. Perhaps the coming months will reveal something that disturbed him in his final days. I have no idea.

I take people as I find, and Dave was a loyal friend to me. The other chaps all thought he was sound, if a tad on the flamboyant side. After we'd all retired, he'd invite us over to his Camelot Castle home for parties, where he kept the friendship ties alive. As the years went by, I saw him more on film than I did in the flesh, but we spoke regularly on the mobiles. Or should I say Dave did, I listened. I will miss his comradeship, humour, cheeky grin and sparkle. See you later, Dave.

Only a few short weeks later Cornish Mick died. He'd made a good age, and he was unwell, but it was still a massive blow. Mick's not going anywhere. That's what I thought. We did things together over a long period of time that he has taken to the grave, and I will too. I kept them out of this book for obvious reasons. I didn't want him or me receiving our birthday telegrams from the King while sitting in a prison cell in a geriatric prison serving a lump. Bless you, Cornish. See you on the other side.

ACKNOWLEDGEMENTS

I'd like to thank my immediate family and loved ones, who I owe my life and ultimate happiness to, and I also pay tribute to my brothers and sisters, who I love dearly and who all shot down the myth that if you have a poor start in life you cannot rise above it. Trevor Booth, my childhood mate, we drifted apart as you do but I hope you're OK, pal, wherever you are. Nick Clark and Tony French, who trusted me on the inside and helped me through my prison years. Pat Sweeney, Terry Munday, Terry Russell, Johnny Forder, Blackie and Winkle – we were great together on the pavement. You've all made your getaway first but I'm bringing up the rear. See you soon, my friends. Mick Cornish, the staunchest man I ever knew. Keep them on their toes, Mick. Freddie Foreman, a wise man and a lovely one. I hope to attend your hundredth birthday party, my friend. Charlie Bronson/Salvador, please God you come out and enjoy your sunset years by the sea painting sunsets. Jon and Andy, for being good friends for so many years now. To Derek, who's seen it all – we keep an eye on one another in our winter years. Del has been encouraging me to do this book for ages. Love ya, Del. Joey Pyle – what can I say? Life has never been the same without you. Thank you for enriching my life. Finally, to all of you who've got this far in the book. Thanks for listening. Hope you enjoyed it.

Ronnie and Martin, 2022